Richard N

M. THERON RANKIN

Apostle of Advance

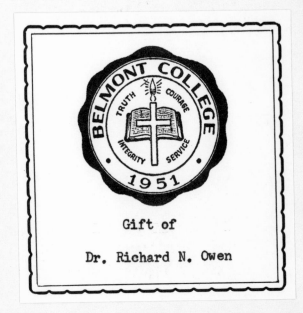

M. Theron Rankin

Apostle of Advance

J. B. Weatherspoon

BROADMAN PRESS
Nashville, Tennessee

424–09039

Library of Congress catalog card number: 58–11550
Printed in the United States of America
4.F58K.S.P.

CONTENTS

DEDICATED
to the
Foreign Missionaries
of the
Southern Baptist Convention

FOREWORD

Theron Rankin and I were friends for many years. When he and his family spent a year in Louisville on their first furlough they worshiped at the Highland Baptist Church where I was pastor. Later, when the Foreign Mission Board invited me to go with Secretary Maddry on a brief mission to the Orient, my wife and I were guests for several weeks in the Rankin home in Canton. After his return to America to live we had many contacts. On his frequent visits to Louisville our home was his headquarters, and we had many hours in which to share experiences.

When I was approached by Mrs. Rankin and the Foreign Mission Board with the suggestion that I write something about him, I hesitated for several reasons. One was that I would have difficulty in keeping anything I might write from becoming a eulogy—so great was my admiration of him. Another was that I did not have the gift or the time for the research necessary for a biography. In the end, however, I consented because I felt so deeply that Dr. Rankin had given a witness and performed a service that deserved to be recorded as a significant chapter in the annals of Southern Baptists.

I have not attempted to write an exhaustive biography, but rather an interpretation of the man—his thoughts, spirit, and vision—as a servant of Jesus Christ. Entertaining episode and anecdote have been secondary to the desire to

1

present the story of his faith, the untiring devotion to his assignments, the tenacious energy and courage with which he carried on amid the tensions and hardships that beset the entire period of his ministry. Without the fanfare of showmanship he traveled far in demonstration of the power of the spirit of Christ within, and came to the end of his life still looking forward. Such a life is worth remembering. And if I have been able to share with others something of the quality of life displayed in his unreserved and burning devotion to Christ in his world purpose, my work has been rewarded in full measure.

I should like to express my thanks to the Foreign Mission Board for making available much material from its files, and to Mrs. Rankin who spent much labor in gathering the material and putting it in my hands. She has given me invaluable assistance. Also I am indebted to G. W. Greene, her brother, for the time he gave in enlightening me on many things; to Dr. Rankin's missionary brother, M. W. Rankin, to his classmate, H. I. Hester, and Hundley Wiley, his fellow missionary, for valuable materials; and to Dr. Eugene Hill of the Foreign Mission Board for his interest and helpfulness. To the editorial staff of the Broadman Press I express appreciation for the care with which they have edited the manuscript.

J. B. WEATHERSPOON

Louisville, Kentucky

I

THE MAKING OF A MISSIONARY

God has a plan for every man's life.

Visibly or invisibly, God girds every man for some exact thing.

The true significance and glory of a man's life is to have achieved the purpose of God for him.

This threefold affirmation of Horace Bushnell's notable sermon expresses the conviction that undergirded Milledge Theron Rankin from the beginning to the end of his career. He learned it first from his father and mother. When in his teens he began to think of his future in the world, the conviction had been rooted firmly in his thought. His decision to become a minister, and later a missionary, rested firmly upon it. Unlike the young man who announced, "I have something I want to say to the world and the pulpit will be my best platform," he accepted his role in the drama of life as a commission from Christ rather than as an outlet for his talents.

It was this sure footing in the purpose of God for his life and the steady tread of full dedication that enabled him to move from faith to larger faith, from strength to greater strength in a spirit of confidence and humility. His simple statement at a critical point of decision in his ministry, "I am a missionary," had all the certainty and finality of Paul's "I am an apostle." And, as with Paul, the claim was not only a defense of his behavior before men but also a constant challenge to his own soul to serve Christ wholly, claiming nothing for himself.

This is the faith and commitment of every true missionary, as of all true servants of Christ. Missionaries differ from one another in gifts and functions, in capacities, in insight and horizon, in temperament and emotional attitudes. In numberless ways individuality shows itself. But they have this in common: a sense of God's purpose and call and a commitment to his service. To say that Theron Rankin stood on this foundation is therefore to say nothing unique, but it is to say something supremely significant—something without which no missionary life can be worthily or effectively built. Without the control and incentive of this conviction —granted to others as one claims it for himself—individuality can make a proud wreck of a man's career and mar the common task. But to interweave one's individuality unselfishly into the common task of a common purpose is to add both strength and beauty to the fabric and to move toward completeness.

Theron Rankin believed and rather remarkably exemplified this. His was not the story of a pioneer who blazed trails into areas not hitherto visited. Nor was it the romance of an individual enterprise that identified his work with his name. He was an appointee of a mission board and a member of a missionary team serving in the framework of corporate decision. He was not a specialist fitted only for a specialized task. By his own choice he went out undesignated for a particular service in order that on the field he might do whatever he was found best fitted to do.

He was not the hero-type of missionary. After his imprisonment by the Japanese a story arose that had him deliber-

4

ately risking his life for a fellow missionary. Essentially the story was true, but he managed to strip it of its heroics. He was simply a missionary and in his own thought never anything else. When he said, "I am a missionary," he not only had reference to his divine commission but also was insisting that his appointment as secretary for the Orient should not destroy his identity with the missionary in the field or place him in a different category.

It was identification with the typical and universal in the missionary calling that won the opportunity for him to introduce into the community of service his distinctive qualities of mind and heart with wholesome effect upon the spirit and fruitfulness of the work. At the same time, it greatly endeared him to his fellow workers and fitted him to become their accepted leader in critical times. In the thirty-two years of his ministry these two convictions appeared repeatedly as the basis and goal of action: the sure calling of God and the brotherly community of the servants of Christ in his redemptive purpose.

What went into his making? How did he arrive at these high convictions? The answer is the wealth of experience in home and church and school and work, a multitude of normal experiences made uncommonly significant by the grace of God and the sincere responsiveness of an alert mind.

The story begins at Newberry, South Carolina. Milledge Theron Rankin was born July 28, 1894, the fourth child and third son of his parents. His father, Milledge Whitfield Rankin (1852–1925), was a Baptist preacher who served various town and country churches in South Carolina through a long ministry. He was a man of fine intelligence and keen spiritual insight, a careful interpreter of the Bible, and beloved for his pastoral faithfulness. He was representative of the large number of Baptist preachers in the South who, without achieving fame or wanting it, shared in keeping strong the foundations of faith and in preparing the way for the remarkable advance of our day. The imperishable heavenly treasures that he gave to hundreds and hundreds of families, whose children were to become the strength of church and community, he imparted also to his own sons and daughters.

Emma Croxton Rankin (1868–1938) was much younger than her husband. As the family grew, her comparative youth and the responsibilities of constant supervision and management meant that her association with the children was more intimately understanding than his. She, as most mothers do and most fathers cannot do, saw and understood and sympathized in the little experiences, in the incipient outcropping of traits and attitudes that needed careful guidance or correction. She could distinguish between mischief and meanness, between steadfastness and stubbornness, and had the common sense and skill to correct one without condoning the other.

She was a devout woman whose mission as mother and minister's wife was adorned by strength of character and full-hearted love as well as unusual ability in household management. When her son Theron, then in China, was told of her death, he wrote to a friend,

I am constantly reminding myself during these days that I have been unusually blessed in my mother. She has given to her children a long, happy and abundant life. God has so abundantly blessed us in the kind of mother he gave us that it does not behoove us as his children to complain when he has seen fit to take her away. The beauty of her life will continue to be an inspiration and source of joy even though she is gone.

Theron shared with his brothers and sisters the guiding and restraining influences of the kind of home life their parents could provide. They did not enjoy opulence or suffer crippling want. The highest salary the preacher-father ever received was a thousand dollars a year; often it was less. The parents and six children (a daughter having died in infancy) had to live, therefore, on a very modest income. From Theron we have this reminiscence in response to an inquiry about the early years:

I cannot recall being conscious to any great extent of the things I did not have. We had so much in the home to make life full and rich that we had little occasion to be concerned about the things we did not have. So long as we were not in physical want, either of food or clothing, which was never the case, we had little to worry about as children.

Now that I have become a man and have a family of my own, I can well understand that my parents had many anxieties from the lack of material resources that we children knew nothing about. I know now that they had to make many sacrifices and had to do much careful planning to make ends meet. They succeeded, however, in giving to their children a sense of security in the home, a security that was not the product primarily of material possessions. We belonged to each other and had the assurance that all of us would help to take care of one another. Each of us drew on the resources of all the others, and each found happiness in sharing his resources with the family. We belonged to an order in which we had implicit confidence. Underneath that sense of confidence and security lay our sense of faith in God. We had confidence in our parents because they believed in God. Through their faith they gave to their children, all seven of us, a heritage which no amount of material possessions could provide. The seven of us together received a heritage sevenfold larger than any one of us could have received by himself. What we received was not something that had to be divided among us, but something that was increased by seven.

7

In such a home Theron Rankin grew up, a healthy, hearty, happy lad, as full of life, fun, mischief, and need of restraint as any other. Such words as *recluse, prodigy,* and *genius* have no place in his biography, certainly not the superlative *meanest,* which he said was necessary for self-protection as the middle child among seven. But there was something about him more valuable than genius for the making of the missionary that he was to become—the good soil of an open, honest, and eager mind.

By the nature of his responsiveness he was habituated in his early years to ways and attitudes that in his maturity would become articulate principles and values central in his living. The following are striking examples: the distinction between material and spiritual values; the meaning of togetherness in a common life and the value of thinking and acting in terms of "we" and "us" rather than "I" and "me"; the dignity of every man; the value of truth and truthfulness; and, centrally, faith in Jesus Christ as the necessary foundation and motivation of life. That they were planted early is the glory of his boyhood home.

The development of life in the environment of a Christian order like the Rankin family was much as would be expected of a vigorous and alert boy. A volume might be written about incidents and episodes that filled life in a large family to the fullest with games and fights, laughter and tears, rebellion and discipline, and with quiet times of prayer and sober counsel; encircling all were the strong bonds of love and loyalty. Life advanced amid the highly educative interplay of personalities.

Personal religious awakening came early to Theron. He publicly confessed his faith in Christ and became a church member before he reached his teens.

His work in school and his growing interests brought from his moderately spoken father the comment, "Theron has a good mind, and it is being well developed." In high school he had his first taste of mental toil motivated by his own interest and initiative. He entered an essay contest on some matter of current public interest. One of his brothers reports that the essay was so much on his mind that he dreamed about it and one night got out of bed to set down some things that had taken shape in his sleep. The project and the fact that he won first prize had creative significance in his personal progress. He found a new interest in learning and in self-expression that turned his thoughts toward further education and his own future. He began to talk about going to college and becoming a lawyer.

In the fall of 1912 he entered Furman University, where he completed a year's work. Because of eye trouble and in order to improve his none-too-secure financial condition, he dropped out of college and worked for a brief period in the post office of his home town. Afterward he went to Durham, North Carolina, where he worked two years in the office of a lumber mill. In order to make good in the responsibilities laid on him in the lumber mill, he studied bookkeeping in a business college at night. This and the practical office experience with financial records and the details of business turned out to be invaluable assets to him in the duties that fell to him later as treasurer of the South China mission, and still later in his secretarial assignments.

Even more important was his spiritual growth, in which he found the true direction his life must take. On his first Sunday in Durham he attended worship at the First Baptist Church, which became, indeed, the house of God and the gate of heaven to him. He did not know that the man who invited him to the service was an angel of God (nor did the man), but it proved to be so. In that church he found an environment and friends that supplied what a youth away from home needed. In the pastor, Dr. John Jeter Hurt, he found a sympathetic counselor and a spiritual father. Theron's sincere manner and faithful attendance not only on Sunday but at the midweek prayer meeting were not unnoticed. Personal contacts established mutual confidence, and before long Dr. Hurt invited him to live in the pastor's home.

In the environment of that second home—full of faith, Christian purpose, and friendly encouragement—Theron's inner life was undergirded. His need for friendly and wholesome social contacts was satisfied. The excellent library of Dr. Hurt was a welcome outlet for his intellectual and religious interests, and established more deeply the habit of reading in which he always would find refreshment and mental stimulation. His religious interests found happy expression in the church where he was encouraged to serve.

It was inevitable that he should face the question of his future. At no time had he thought of his present employment as anything but an interim necessity. In high school he had dreamed of being a lawyer. But now with his increasing religious consciousness, which had been so richly nurtured by experiences since his conversion, another possibility came into the picture—the Christian ministry. It came to him as a personal question to be resolved, not by a self-estimate of his ability or by personal preference, but by a conviction of the purpose and will of God. In the seclusion of his own thought and prayer he searched for the answer and found it. He must be a minister.

One thing remained to cast a shadow of uncertainty on his decision—the problem of "bread." Preparation for the ministry was a long road, and he had little money. How could he even begin it? He confided his conviction and his problem to his pastor, who again with true Christian understanding came to his side with reassurance and practical help. By obtaining the assistance of a layman, Dr. Hurt paved the way for Theron to enter Wake Forest College in 1915.

In college Theron soon was making his own way. One of his employments, which proved during his imprisonment years in Hong Kong to have been a valuable experience, was in the kitchen where he shared in cooking. Later he became a student pastor in rural churches, serving Christ, gaining practical experience, and, incidentally, making a living. At the same time he was quite active in extracurricular activities that were to his liking. One of his chief interests was the literary society, which was an important part of college life. Although he never aspired to the grand style of the orator, his logic, his clearness and accuracy of statement, his directness and skill in the use of facts won him an honored place on the college debating teams. He also enjoyed tennis, which he kept up for many years, gathering a rather large collection of trophies in his early missionary years.

As a student he stood well within the honor bracket, maintaining a high average throughout his course. Asked later by the Foreign Mission Board for his estimate of Rankin's ability, one of his college professors wrote, "I offered him my work as college teacher during my leave of absence," and added, "In my opinion he is a perfect and true Christian gentleman, earnest and reliable." High qualities of character and solid intellectual ability were his twin marks of distinction. After three years he was graduated with honor.

Declining an invitation to become a pastor in South Carolina, Theron entered the Southern Baptist Theological Seminary in the fall of 1918 and three years later received his Master of Theology degree, having made an even better record than in college.

It was in his second year in the seminary that he decided to be a missionary. One providential factor in that decision was the fact that in his early home life and in his father's preaching he had been made conscious of missions as an integral part of Christian service. Reading the missionary literature that came to the home made the missionary and his work into living pictures.

Another factor was the prominence of missionary emphasis in the seminary. There biblical study, historical and theological, made clear and emphatic the universal redemptive purpose of God in Jesus Christ and the world mission of the church. Once a month classes were suspended and the whole student body was converted into a "society for missionary inquiry." In the chapel he heard informing missionary addresses, letters from missionaries, and challenges to face personally the question of one's own field of service. From the earliest history of the seminary there had been a steady stream of graduates to work in foreign fields. Rankin was too sincere a student to refuse to face the personal question that was sure to be raised.

Still another factor was one that is not present with all students. Also to Louisville in the fall of 1918 came Miss Valleria Greene, a daughter of missionaries to China, as a student in the Woman's Missionary Union Training School. They soon met and became friends. Among other things they talked much about China and the Chinese people and the life of missionaries. The result was much more than increased knowledge of China and a quickened interest in missions—Rankin fell in love.

On a Missionary Day at the seminary in his second year, after an address by Dr. Eugene Sallee, a missionary to China, Rankin went forward dedicating his life to missionary service. His hope-lifting joy was to learn later in the day that Valleria Greene had gone down another aisle, reaffirming her own dedication! Each had gone without knowledge of the other's intention. Truly God moves in mysterious, and often delightful, ways to work out his will for human lives. Soon these two in mutual love had decided to serve together, and none who knows the wonderful life they had together can doubt that God was leading all the way.

Thus young people are made missionaries. The roads of preparation are not identical, but in all cases a multitude of factors by the grace and providence of God combine to make plain the path of his choosing. Miss Greene graduated from the Training School in May, 1920, and by appointment of the Southern Baptist Foreign Mission Board went to China a few months later. Theron Rankin, having won his theological degree, followed a year later in full certainty of God's good pleasure and with happier anticipations than are given to most.

> There is one way for thee; but one; inform
> Thyself of it; pursue it; one way each
> Soul hath by which the infinite in reach
> Lieth before him; seek and ye shall find.
> . . . .
> Thou hast thy way to go, thou hast thy day
> To live; thou hast thy need of thee to make
> In the hearts of others; do thy thing; yes, slake
> The world's thirst for yet another man!
> And be thou sure of this: no other can
> Do for thee that appointed thee of God. *

* R. W. Dixon, as quoted in James A. Robertson's *The Divine Vocation in Human Life.*

II

APPRENTICESHIP IN SOUTH CHINA
1921–27

World War I aroused America to a new consciousness of the world. With all its hatred and horror, the conflict of nations dealt a deathblow to isolation. We were in the world. Although reluctant at the first to accept its full political responsibility, our nation was unable to escape either the international bonds or the cost of ignoring their meaning.

Christian America shared the new consciousness and saw as never before the world's need of Christ. Leaders began to urge upon the churches the Christian responsibility for an immediate expansion of the missionary enterprise. The major Christian denominations and other groups undertook to raise hitherto undreamed-of amounts of money and to challenge young Christians to dedicate their lives to foreign service. The Southern Baptist Convention launched a campaign to raise seventy-five million dollars for its world mission program. By 1921, the second year of the undertaking, the tide of money and missionary volunteers had reached unprecedented proportions. At its June meeting that year the Foreign Mission Board appointed forty-seven candidates in a single day. It was a new day for foreign missions. The Christian forces of the nation were up in arms; the slogan "the moral equivalent of war" was revived as hundreds of young men and women enlisted under the command of Christ.

Among those appointed in 1921 was Theron Rankin. He

was chosen for the South China Mission to sail as soon as arrangements could be made. Only those who have had the experience can imagine the tension and excitement of the next few weeks. There were a thousand and one things to be done; many "good-bys" to be said to friends and relatives; hallowed days at home with his mother, brothers and sisters, and with his father, whose face he would not see again. It is revealing to note that he was not too busy to pay a farewell visit to the Baptist church at Simpsonville, Kentucky, where he had been student pastor while in the seminary; and to Dr. J. J. Hurt and his family, then residing in Wilmington, North Carolina. These friends had played significant parts in his preparation for his life's work, and letters would not suffice to express his gratitude and love. Such visits as these were repeated throughout his life at intervals when he had opportunity. This quality of appreciation, not only of what people had done for him but also of what they were, expressed more in quiet action than in words, made friends and kept them wherever he worked.

With a large group of missionaries, sixty of whom were Baptists, he embarked on the *Hawk Eye* for the Orient on July 15, 1921. The three weeks at sea were spent in reading important books about the Chinese people and in the fellowship of other missionaries, of whom he had many questions to ask. One fellow traveler remarked, "M. T. Rankin is on his way to becoming a Baptist with a well-stocked mind." When the shore line of Japan was sighted with the towering Fujiyama in the background, his companion on deck, admiring the beauty, said, "You will not find the China shore line as beautiful as this." In reply the young missionary revealed where his chief interest lay. He answered, "Tell me more about the Chinese people."

His destination was Canton, where he was to be identified with the South China Mission. The mission included all the appointed missionaries of the Foreign Mission Board in the two provinces of Kwangtung and Kwangsi. In 1921 there were about seventy members serving in twelve stations or centers stretching across many miles and embracing millions of China's population. Canton was the oldest and largest of the stations, the center of Chinese Baptist work in South China.

In a section of the city called Tungshan was a remarkable, even unique, community of Baptist institutions, including a kindergarten, elementary and middle schools for boys and girls, a hospital, an orphanage, an old people's home, a school for the blind, a training school for Christian women, a theological seminary, a publishing house, and the wonderful Tungshan Baptist Church. The homes of the missionaries were there, as also was the headquarters building of the Leung Kwang Baptist Association. This was an organization of Baptists covering the two provinces, Kwangtung and Kwangsi. Although in close co-operation with the missionaries and the mission, it was as autonomous as the Southern Baptist Convention. When the writer was in Canton in 1935 the association had assumed full responsibility for such institutions as those in Canton and was conducting a vigorous program of evangelism, education, and social ministries in a broad area.

In such a community as this and with the many benefits of accumulated experience, the young missionary might face confidently the tasks of orientation and apprenticeship. Nevertheless, there are in every instance unavoidable testings. No previous study, no bright anticipations can deliver a person from unexpected challenges of faith and purpose.

Theron Rankin was no exception. Nor was his fiancée, Miss Valleria Greene, who had preceded him a year before. One of the visions that gladdened their prospect was destined to be hidden behind a cloud.

They were expecting to be married as soon as Theron arrived, but the wedding had to be postponed because she was ill. In the months of waiting both of them were tried to the depths. She on her part had to face the whole question of her future. Should she try to remain as a missionary in Canton or move to another climate? To the problem of her health was added another that she had not anticipated a year before but must now face seriously—whether or not she should marry the young missionary. In the situation he too faced the deepest questions: Why am I here? Am I here because I fell in love with Miss Greene, or because God called me and wants me in this place? Finally the answer was clear: Whatever happens, I shall remain and do my work because it is the will of God for me. To his unbounded joy he soon learned that (as had happened in their dedication) Miss Greene had at about the same time found the answer in her own heart—she too would remain and marry him! In one set of circumstances or another every young missionary has to face the question, Why am I here? And if he is to do his best work, the reason must be one from which there is no turning back.

They were married in the spring of 1922 and for more than thirty years worked together in the service of Christ. With a rare congeniality of thought, temperament, and outlook they were equal partners in an illustrious ministry. In Canton Mrs. Rankin taught with her mother Mrs. G. W. Greene (whom she succeeded as principal) in the Bible Training School for Women (*Pooi In*), where she did immeasurable service in preparing women to be witnesses and teachers. These in turn would train others to be witnesses.

Among the major disciplines of the young missionary is language study. It is his first assignment. In China it sentenced Theron the first year to hard labor—five hours a day and five days a week. It was his one job. The roseate colors in the picture of a missionary life suddenly became drab. The apostolic injunction began to speak with fresh imperative: "Make every effort to supplement your faith with virtue, and virtue with knowledge, and knowledge with self-control, and self-control with steadfastness." One had to be content to grind away at elementary things and wait, while others went on preaching, teaching, and testifying. A small hint of his inward struggle is given in a letter to Dr. T. B. Ray of the Foreign Mission Board at the end of the first year: "I am longing for the time to come when I shall be able to add something to the efforts of our workers. For the present I can only learn—and there is so very, very much to learn."

In his language study Rankin had better advantages than most enjoy. He was a superior language student, having made his highest grades in both college and seminary in that field, including English, Latin, German, Greek, and Hebrew. He also had the help of Mrs. Rankin, who was born in China and grew up to speak Chinese naturally. Her only difficulty was the limitation of her English vocabulary. One day they came upon a group of Chinese quarreling as only Chinese can quarrel; words flew like bullets. Theron exclaimed, "Do you know what they are saying?" His wife's reply was, "Yes, I know, but I don't know the English for it." For ordinary language, however, she was as adept as a native in both languages, which made her progress much easier. In the letter quoted he also wrote,

I have passed my first year's examination in the language, and have all my plans for taking up my second year's work. During the past year I have kept myself free from all other work and am planning to keep myself free from any responsible work during the second year. I hope to take several trips into the country in evangelistic work in order to practice the language I have learned and to learn the work. I am fully convinced that a good grasp of the language is fundamental to good work.

Mrs. Rankin's missionary brother, G. W. (Bill) Greene, initiated him into preaching. Bill often was called upon as an interpreter. He was Rankin's interpreter in his first sermon and often thereafter. He says of their experience together,

I always liked to talk over with the speaker beforehand the talk which he planned to make. Theron was most cooperative and asked many questions, seeking light upon the technics of such an operation. He was particularly interested in avoiding difficulties. There are many of them. I worked with him a great deal and he soon became expert in preaching sermons which lent themselves to putting into Chinese. He used the Bible a great deal but was always careful not to make allusions to it that would be meaningless to those not well acquainted with it. Other literary allusions he studiously avoided. His illustrations were also carefully chosen and used freely and effectively.

In addition to this free help, he had, of course, an expert Chinese language teacher who provided the grind of daily study. He wrote to the secretary further, "I am hoping that my work will be such that I can take the third year's work in language." He was willing to make haste slowly in order that he might be able to communicate the gospel more effectively to the people in their own terms and patterns.

Besides the language he was learning constantly the spirit, program, and methods of the South China Mission. Organized with a chairman, secretary, treasurer, and executive committee, the mission was the Foreign Mission Board's medium of administration in that area. It served as a council and clearinghouse for the varied and interrelated activities of the missionaries. At its meetings reports from the several stations were made; difficulties and needs were discussed; suggestions as to policies and programs to be recommended to the Board were considered.

At first the meetings of the mission brought to the observant young missionary a certain disillusionment. He had anticipated an undisturbed harmony. Instead he listened to debates in which here and there appeared strong personal feelings—sometimes between members of the same station—as men urged the importance of their own particular ideas, tasks, and projects and with difficulty yielded to the common judgment of the mission as to undertakings and methods. He saw men behaving abroad much as they did at home. Individuality had difficulty in finding common ground with community. Here was something with which he would have to live, but only as an evident fact that pained him.

On the other hand, his association with the missionaries and with the Christian community in Canton undergirded him with a fellowship of understanding and sympathy. And the meetings of the mission were not all disillusionment. They renewed perspectives and kept alive the sense of unity. Through the mission the individual missionary received spiritual reinforcement. The truth was not quite as the little boy thought who, when asked what the mission meeting was,

20

replied, "That is where you get down and pray, and then you get up and fight."

Through such experiences the young missionary became aware that being missionaries does not exempt men from the common difficulties of living together, that co-operation is a demanding enterprise, and that harmonious relations even among men committed to the work of Christ can be achieved only by a constant pursuit by each one of "godliness . . . brotherly affection . . . and love." He also felt the benefits of community so deeply in his own experience and prized it so highly that it became one of the chief goals of his missionary career. His orientation to missionary work in South China did much to establish his concept of the Christian life as being individual-in-community. He experienced a growing conviction that strong individuality—strong in faith, character, and thought—merging itself into a strong community—strong in mutual esteem, purpose, and organization—was the only way of progress in the missionary task.

Another element of orientation came through contact with the Chinese people. In the Tungshan community in Canton he saw the rich fruitage of missions. In the milling thousands in the streets of the city he saw enough to stir his compassion for the lost. As he accompanied the workers in their chapel work, his heart was drawn toward direct evangelism as his part. He was soon introduced to rural China where he saw the grass roots of the plodding and spiritually lost nation.

Before he could speak at all in Chinese, G. W. Greene took him on a trip which introduced him to the rigors as well as the values of rural evangelism. They went up the Bamboo River several hundred miles from Canton to visit a number of churches and chapels. Mr. Greene describes some of the more amusing and trying experiences of the trip. They found the Chinese boat very crowded, and soon, the atmosphere having become unbearable, they decided to go out on top, where for a while all was pleasant. Then it began to rain. The boat people called them to come below, but they chose the rain. There they sat—and sang! Below someone remarked, "Those two certainly are very *kum lam*" (that is, are able to take a lot of soaking), many times later a useful phrase for what a missionary must have to weather a variety of inconveniences and obstacles.

Later on when they were far up in the country, Greene came down with flu, which was no comfort to the beginner. They were in a Chinese inn, and sleep was none too sound. In the middle of the night Rankin, awakened by a strange commotion in the room, cried out, "Bill, what in the world is that?" After a moment the old hand assured him it was nothing dangerous, only some pigs rooting around under the bed. The return home was safe enough, but not without apprehension. The first fifty miles were made in a small boat. Greene reports, "We made the trip in good order and caught the last steamboat of the season. While in the small boat we were stopped several times, and I got out and went to parley with the robbers. Except for some 'tea money' which we had to give them we made the trip O. K. Later we went back and visited other churches and chapels."

But adventure and discomfort were marginal to the essential value of this and other such experiences. They revealed more and more of the many-sided China. They deepened Rankin's sympathy and his admiration of the patience and strength of the Chinese people. It was in a little rural church that he had what he called his richest personal experience in soul-winning.

It came some time after I reached China. Months had been spent studying the Chinese, and I was still scarcely able to make myself understood. One night at a country church I was asked to give a brief message in the beginning of the service. It was haltingly spoken and the invitation was hesitatingly given. But a ten-year-old boy came forward confessing Christ as his Savior. I had gone to China to give my life to help win people to Christ and that night I had the experience of winning my first Chinese for him.

He recalled other experiences such as winning an old woman to a joyous and confident faith, and also a student who, desiring to learn English, was helping him read the Chinese New Testament; but the greatest thrill, "my richest personal experience at soul-winning," was the first. He had become a real missionary!

The year 1923 was a well-marked milestone. In a letter to Dr. T. B. Ray in February he made two triumphant announcements. One was that he had passed another examination in language study. The other was of the birth of their first child, Valleria Page Rankin. The mood he was in is reflected in the addendum,

Of course we think the little lady is very wonderful—but not so wonderful as Elizabeth's and Hun's (the Wileys in Shanghai), since a recent letter from Elizabeth announced the amazing fact that their girl is gaining at the amazing rate of eight pounds a week. We hope she intended to write *ounces;* else we fear for the health of those who have to care for such a charge.

Also by the spring of 1923 his apprenticeship had so far proved his ability as to warrant his appointment to important duties in the educational program in Canton. He was asked to serve on the newly instituted board of trustees of

the girls' school, Pooi To; and to become a teacher in the
Graves Theological Seminary, his assignments being a New
Testament course in Chinese and courses in Greek, Old
Testament, and Comparative Religion in English for stu-
dents who understood English.

In the earlier years the girls' school, which was established
by the missionaries, was under their management. In the
course of time as the Chinese Christian community developed, Chinese were invited to share in its direction and support. It remained, however, more a school of the mission than
of the Chinese. The Chinese were therefore rather indifferent to their responsibilities, feeling that their relation was
little more than nominal. By the 1920's the situation was far
from satisfactory and the school was in straits. A solution
was sought in the appointment of an autonomous board of
trustees composed of selected missionaries and Chinese with
a Chinese chairman, thus paving the way for it to become an
accepted enterprise of the Leung Kwang Baptist Association.
Rankin was selected as one of its members.

Sometime later he wrote to the Board, "The Chinese
members of the committee seem to feel that they have a real
part in the management of the school, and yet I could see
no tendency whatever to 'run away' with authority. I think
we are on the road to clearing up the trouble which has
been standing so long." Of his own participation he said, "As
an inexperienced missionary I have felt quite a hesitancy in
assuming the responsibility of a member of the committee,
but it seems probable that the very fact of our short experience will enable us to accomplish results which we probably
could not had we been here longer." In this early experience
he had a taste of the meaning and worth of promoting indigenous Christianity, which lay firmly in the policy of the

24

South China Mission. The people of a nation should be free to evangelize and Christianize and to develop their institutions. The role of the missionary, he came to see, is that of counselor and helper.

The professorship in the seminary was accepted with some reluctance. It meant a choice between concentrating his ministry on a comparatively few students and answering the desire of his heart to be an evangelist. Although he had gone out uncommitted to any particular kind of work, he soon felt the tug of the great numbers in Canton who needed the gospel, and as with the other missionaries he visualized the possibilities, he was drawn to give himself to an advanced evangelistic undertaking. Months before he had written to his former roommate and very close friend, H. I. Hester:

I am trying to look about and decide what kind of work I can best do. I am now thinking strongly of doing evangelistic work in the city of Canton. It is the plan of our mission to develop a large evangelistic center in the city and to put up something on the order of an institutional church. In addition to this central point we would have chapels all about the city where services would be held daily. We would have a good force of native preachers and Bible women working with the people. There is a wonderful opportunity for such a work. There are thousands and thousands of people in Canton who know practically nothing about Christianity. I am turning more and more away from the idea of teaching in the seminary.

When the shortage of teachers and the judgment of the Board and mission seemed to make acceptance imperative, he still felt his inadequacy. He wrote, "I feel very strongly that one should have considerable experience in itinerating preaching before one is fitted to teach others to preach." With that in mind he continued his evangelistic ministry in

25

Canton and beyond. Although he was busy in the summer of 1923 preparing for his seminary duties plus "the job of having the buildings of one of our schools put into good condition and the job of overseeing the grading of some of our property," he did not omit "itinerating preaching." He wrote, "I have several chapels in the country which I want to visit during the summer."

In May, 1924, he wrote a long letter to Dr. Ellis A. Fuller from "somewhere in China," describing one of his preaching tours en route. At the end of the letter he wrote, "I hope I can get a boat down, for I have walked about 125 miles." The purpose was to visit the little churches in the back country from Shiuhing, preaching and evangelizing and at the same time exploring needs that the mission might be able to meet. Only a few excerpts from the letter must suffice to tell of the rigors and richness of the experience.

On the following day (after a brief visit at Shiuhing with the missionaries, Misses Shumate and Gunn) I walked seven miles out to a place called New Bridge where representatives from the churches and chapels of this section were meeting—we should call it an "associational meeting" at home. Miss Shumate had preceded me. We had a great three days' meeting there. Among other things the "association" voted to open a book store in Shiuhing. Seven hundred and fifty dollars were needed. Dr. Cheung, a physician and church leader, was asking for gifts. He began with a hundred dollars. This was increased by the congregation to $250, and then it seemed that a standstill had been reached. After a considerable wait Dr. Cheung offered to give half of the remaining $500 if the others would raise the balance. Everyone strained to the utmost, many of the people doubling their original gifts. Most of them were preachers who got about $25 a month. At last only about $39 remained, but everyone felt that he had paid the last possible dollar. Finally, a young layman who had already made two pledges arose and said that he had

M. Theron Rankin

Valleria Greene Rankin

given every cent he could pay, but he had on an overcoat which had cost him more than the balance wanted. It was practically new. He would give it for the balance if it could be sold for the balance. Dr. Cheung at once accepted the coat for the balance. Next morning I saw the young man without his coat—he had already sent it to Canton to be sold. Just a few years ago this man was a wild fellow and very much opposed to Christianity. He was a very strong "controverter," and in order to be able to argue more intelligently he made a study of the Bible. The Bible out-argued him, and this is a part of the results.

It was such qualities of faith that helped to create an unbounded admiration for the Chinese Christians and confidence in their ability to advance the gospel.

On the day following this meeting,

Miss Shumate, a Bible woman, a Chinese pastor and I started out on the first lap of our trip. We walked five miles to a place called "White Pig," arriving about ten o'clock in the morning. It was market day in the village and a large number of people were there. We opened the chapel and put out a board announcing services, one at one o'clock and another at seven. We had good crowds at both services. I made an effort to preach both times and had a fine hearing. After the services a number remained to talk about the gospel. On Saturday night we visited the nearby villages and did personal work among the people. I talked with several poor old opium smokers who were interested in becoming Christians, but could not muster the strength to quit their opium. Another one we talked with has only recently quit and promised us that he would join the church at the next day for the Lord's Supper. He was converted more than a year before. On Sunday I preached twice again and had people in my room almost all the time between services talking about the gospel.

On Monday they walked nine miles to Yiu Kwoo, where they had a dinner of boiled sweet potatoes. In the afternoon

27

Rankin walked with the local pastor to a near-by village to see a brother Christian. The good man "urged me to stay for the afternoon meal, promising me a good fat puppy, which he showed me running about the yard, if I would stay. I have always been a lover of dogs, but I love them alive too much to care for them served at table. I declined." Returning to Yiu Kwoo he preached in the chapel in the evening. "The house was crowded, and the people listened as children listen to a story."

Several days later,

We made eighteen miles today and then had a walk over the city after we got in. We are up here where foreigners are seldom seen. I am quite a curiosity. We are in a district city tonight, which is the governing city for this area. We will use this as headquarters from which to make four other outlying points. We are in the land of robbers here. Tomorrow night we plan to spend the night in a village twelve miles out, which we hear was robbed five nights ago. But I suspect we will be the safer there because the robbers will not come back so quickly. We shall go on about ten miles farther up the next day to the farthest preaching station we have up in this country. I am the first foreign preacher to visit up here in twelve years.

Still later,

We walked about nine miles yesterday away from the river, the only road in this country, and then crossed over a range of mountains over two thousand feet high. Then we dropped down into a little valley to a small village, all the houses of which are made of mud, with bark roofs. Here we spent the night. I slept in the same room with a cow, chickens, ducks and a dog. The only reason a pig was not there was that the man had no pig. They have to keep all their provisions in the house or the robbers will get them. We hear of the operation of these robbers on every hand.

I am the first foreign man who has ever been here. Miss Shumate has been here before, the only foreign woman and first foreign person to come. We are about as far removed from modern civilization, in its effects, as it is possible to be. If Confucius had died here and were to come to life now, all he would have to do would be to say "good morning" and take up his conversation where he left off. And yet the light of the gospel is here. About ten years ago the leading man in the village was converted. By the time he joined the church his two brothers were converted. A total of more than twenty converts in three villages are the results of the lives and testimony of these first three men.

Any account of these early years of digging in would be incomplete without a reference to the political and social climate. The word that describes it is "revolution." Indeed, that is the word that fits the entire period of Rankin's ministry. Kenneth Scott Latourette in his book *A Short History of the Far East* has said that in the five decades after 1895 China was passing through five revolutions—political, intellectual, religious, economic, and social—and "in so doing she was telescoping into half a century the changes which in Europe had required six centuries." Added to radical internal changes were the Japanese invasion, World War II, and the Communist triumph. Latourette vividly describes the history of missions during this period as "advance through storm."

Rankin had been in Canton less than a year when open fighting was renewed in South China. A general in Canton, defecting to the northern regime, attempted a *coup d'état* while Sun Yat-sen and his army were away, resulting in the heavy bombardment of the city by Dr. Sun's returning forces before it was retaken and order restored. Some of the missionaries in the untouched Tungshan area watched its bombardment from their housetops. Such violent eruptions were a part of the titanic struggle going on in the whole nation, a struggle between radically different concepts of life which would determine the nation's future. The missionaries were conscious of this, and although like the masses of Chinese they were able for the most part to pursue their daily tasks without much interruption, they knew that the work of missions would be tried to the roots by what was going on. References to the situation were often in Rankin's letters. Further anxieties were added to their tensions and questionings in 1923 when Russian Communists (Borodin and others) appeared in Canton as friendly advisers of Dr. Sun.

Even though Sun Yat-sen, who was a Christian, was sympathetic with their evangelical purpose, they knew well his political principles could not leave the missionary enterprise unaffected. His principle of nationalism, although not directly antiforeign, called for national autonomy and freedom from foreign domination. Foreign missions could not escape being associated with foreign governments and foreign commercial enterprise. The principle of democracy, which envisaged the ultimate (but not immediate) control of the government by the people, would be applied increasingly to educational and religious institutions. The principle of the people's livelihood offered to the people an economic and social hope that played, even more than the first two, into the hands of the Communists. After Dr. Sun's death in 1925 his party, the Kuo-min-tang, elevated him to the level of national saint and made these principles its bible. The Christian fear was deepened when immediately left-wingers, under the leadership of Communist Borodin, took the initiative in an antiforeign, anti-Christian interpretation of the party program.

30

At the height of the early Communist influence in Canton Rankin and a few other missionaries sought and obtained an interview with Borodin and a group of Communist leaders. They felt that the antagonism toward the missionaries was due in part to misunderstanding and that it might be worth while to try to explain the objectives and motives of Christian missions in China. Their action was a display not only of strength and courage but also of a certain respect for human reasonableness. In a later reference to the interview Rankin revealed a trait familiar to all who worked with him —his effort always to understand the other man's point of view, which emptied many a conflict of bitterness and despising. He said,

As we talked I saw from the reactions of this man [Borodin] that he was hearing ideas he had never heard before. And I caught myself wishing that I could get behind that forehead of his and see through his eyes and his mind as he saw. I thought of Greek Catholicism in Russia, and the days of the Czars. I tried to picture for myself the conception that man had gained of Christianity from those who called themselves Christian. And I was convinced of this, that if Christianity were actually and truly what that man thought it was, I would be an atheist too.

The influence of the Communists added a sinister and portentous quality to that of the revolutionary changes already taking place. Communism was especially attractive to the student population and did not halt at the gate of the Christian schools. "For a time in the 1920's and the 1930's many of the ablest and most intellectual of the students of China were attracted by Communism because it seemed to promise a quick and decisive attack on the problems of the country. Many of the Christian students appeared to be un-

certain and uninformed on the basic tenets of their faith."
In Canton the receptive, even eager, attitude that the young
missionary had noticed in 1921 and 1922 was soon giving
way to caution and suspicion. The secular education of the
new Chinese thought, with "science" as the magic word,
raised questions concerning the religious emphasis of the
Christian schools. The educational leadership of the missionaries lost in respect. This was true in the Graves Theological
Seminary as well. The restlessness, the critical and unwhole-
some attitudes, the uncertainty among a number of students
so deeply grieved the president that he felt he should resign.

In 1925 Rankin was asked to become president of the seminary. He was in agreement with the growing idea that a
Chinese properly should be president and accepted only because there was no able Chinese leader available at the time.

Meeting the situation so intimately, first as teacher and
then as president, it was necessary for him to make a careful
and sympathetic appraisal of the students' problems. Their
attitudes were hard to reconcile with their Christian faith,
and the situation could not be changed in a day. The number of students was declining. The service of the institution
was hampered greatly, so much so that the question of continuing was raised. Those befuddled young men needed the
seminary, however; they needed to see the meaning of
Christ, to possess the truth not as something from the West
but from God, with a meaning for China and a bearing upon
life in the new order more imperative than any philosophy
of man.

Moreover, the future of the Christian movement in China
needed the seminary. There must be leaders—pastors, teachers, principals and presidents, administrators of institutions
—who, if there was to be any steadfastness, must not only

know that they were Christians, but why. The worth-while-ness of the seminary was not to be measured in terms of easy conformity of the student mind or the size of the student body but in terms of need and purpose and the harvest of well-taught men, however few, who would go out to be strong servants of the kingdom of God. With the courage of that conviction Rankin for the next two years (until furlough time) taught and toiled at that chief task. His experiences, largely unreported, lacked much of the thrill his evangelistic heart desired but yielded the satisfaction of making a deposit in a strong Chinese ministry and church life without which evangelism would go limping.

So by the end of his first term of service (which is considered by the Foreign Mission Board to be a period of probation), Theron Rankin had been introduced to the realities of missionary life. He had served well in his apprenticeship and had merited responsible assignments. He had found among the missionaries with whom he worked a fellowship that he loved and in which he was loved. His missionary world had expanded in its outward proportions and inwardly in its spiritual demands. The missionary life was not so simple as he had dreamed. He was conscious of more problems than he had started with, more conscious of the necessity laid upon him by Jesus Christ.

III

A YEAR IN AMERICA
1927–28

In the summer of 1927 Rankin returned to America on furlough for one year. He and Mrs. Rankin and their little daughter "Pagie" settled in Louisville in a shady nook called Wildwood, near the Southern Baptist Theological Seminary. It was an ideal spot for their purposes of quietude, rest, and study.

The year was dotted with deputation work—both he and Mrs. Rankin being much sought after by the churches—and occasional visits to friends and relatives. The main business, however, was further preparation for the work in China. The six years had yielded a store of experience that needed to be straightened out in his mind. He had encountered a world that was rapidly and radically changing. There were trends in politics and government, in education and social attitudes that created new and serious problems for the missionary. Established concepts of the missionary task and methods were being challenged at many points. Changing relations with the government, the growth of Chinese churches and institutions and the increasing role of Chinese Christian leadership, the progressive movement toward interdenominational co-operation, the increasing antipathy toward things foreign and Western—these and other trends required careful evaluation in their bearings upon missionary policy.

For guidance in facing these problems Rankin returned

to the seminary and to Dr. W. O. Carver, the seminary's philosopher and historian of missions. Upon Dr. Carver's advice the course of his study was laid out. He chose the National Christian Council of China for special study and for the theme of his doctoral dissertation. The wisdom of this study lay first in the fact that it would give a more comprehensive view of the missionary task as it was interpreted by widely representative leaders. It would help also in evaluating more accurately on the basis of fact the work of the council in relation to Baptist missions and the total missionary enterprise. Still further, it would give a better understanding of the general ecumenical movement which took shape in the early 1900's and whose influence was felt everywhere.

In 1913 the Continuation Committee of the World Missionary Conference (Edinburgh, 1910) held five area conferences in China, which led to the organization of a Chinese Continuation Committee. This committee was composed of sixty members, of whom one third were Chinese. Its purpose was to further the missionary enterprise by establishing communication among the various Christian groups and to become a clearinghouse of opinion concerning the missionary task and procedures. In 1922 the work of this committee issued in the organization of the National Christian Council of a hundred members, a majority to be Chinese, representing various denominational and nondenominational evangelical groups; this council was to pursue and expand the work of the former committee.

By 1927 the Council was proving to be a vigorous and powerful influence in the whole Christian movement. The Chinese majority in its membership gave it prestige among Chinese Christians. Organized on a voluntary co-operative, rather than federative or unitive, basis, and excluding from its concern all doctrinal and ecclesiastical matters, it invited the participation of widely different groups. Moreover, its actual service through counsel and widely distributed information was contributing much toward the understanding of the over-all task and toward friendly relations among Christians, foreign and Chinese.

This movement claimed the attention of every alert Southern Baptist missionary. It raised in a new context questions concerning denominational relations and attitudes, co-operation and the limits of co-operation; questions concerning the role of the foreign mission and missionaries in relation to the Chinese churches and Chinese leadership; and questions concerning traditional missionary objectives and new directions for missionary work. New conditions and new proposals made it necessary to face these questions seriously. That Rankin undertook to do.

His doctoral thesis is a report of his investigation and critical evaluation. Our biographical interest does not call for a full review of its contents. It is sufficient to say that it represents a thorough, and one may say sympathetic, study of the originating factors, aims, program, attainments, and tendencies of the movement. Our chief interest is not even in the conclusions he reached about the Council but rather in the qualities of mind, the insights, convictions, and attitudes revealed that would give strength and trustworthiness to his leadership in the critical times ahead.

For one thing, he revealed an attitude that showed fitness to deal with problems that emerged from the frustrations of the time and for which there was no easy or unanimous solution. He was keen to observe, ready to listen, patient to understand, and willing for his own thought to be challenged. His was akin to the attitude of W. L. Watkinson, who, when a friend expressed dismay at finding him reading Nietzsche, replied, "I love to read Nietzsche; he challenges everything I believe." His interest was not determined by agreement or disagreement. This was demonstrated in his undertaking to learn all he could about the co-operative movement in China. It was hailed by some as the only solution for Christianity's problems in the world. By others it was heartily condemned as an ambitious interloper. Rankin chose to regard it not as something sinister but as a serious proposal for the Christianization of China and, therefore, worthy of being understood. He wrote, "I have attempted to make this examination from a nonpartisan point of view. I have had no theory concerning the Council to prove."

He demonstrated also a quality of thoroughness. He was not content to hear one side of a story or to approach a problem from one angle. He refused to jump to conclusions. It was this quality of thoroughness that in the future would win him respect and make his arguments and judgments so often convincing. His procedure in regard to the National Council was first to review the changes that had taken place in the recent past in the national life of China and in the Christian movement in China as they were related to the missionary task; then to study the analysis of the missionary task made by the proponents of the Council and on the basis of which the aims and program of the Council were launched; next to examine the stated aims of the Council, its organization, its program, and its work up to 1927; and finally to make a critical evaluation of the achievements of the movement and the direction in which it was moving. The criteria for his evaluation were the basic concepts of the Christian faith and purpose that he held.

In this critical evaluation, and at points earlier in the

study, another important element of strength appears: his understanding of basic Christianity and the discernment with which he brought missionary aims and methods under the light of Christian principles.

In the constitution of the National Council there was no statement of theological or ecclesiological tenets. It presented to the Christian groups in China a statement of aims and proposed a method of procedure. All groups (and individuals) were free to examine them and to decide whether or not they were compatible with their own principles of faith. So Rankin brought to his study his own basic concepts, which were also those held by Baptists generally. Nowhere formally stated by him, such concepts as the following appear as bases of judgment: the supreme authority of Christ and his teaching; religion as a personal experience; the dignity and responsibility of the individual; the brotherhood of all believers; the freedom and responsibility of every local church; the freedom of association of individuals and churches in the service of Christ; and the universal redemptive purpose of Christ working by the Holy Spirit and through the church, which is his body.

Examining the Council's statement of its aims in the light of these concepts, he was frank to say that he saw no essential conflict. For example, the aim to "promote spiritual unity among the followers of Christ in China" has full support in the prayer of our Lord. "It is one for which we all should pray and work with an earnestness which Christ manifested for this oneness." He was conscious that certain interpretations of unity and tendencies by individual leaders endangered the whole effort, but he wrote, "We must recognize here that the aims of the Council itself are in the right direction."

Again, the aim of promoting indigenous (i.e., self-directing, self-propagating, and self-supporting) churches in China was in accord with the faith and policy of Baptists. The right to be free and independent was as true of a church in China as in America. The achievement of this presented many problems, but the aim rested on fundamental truth. Nor did he have any quarrel with the aim of a more comprehensive understanding and effort in relation to the missionary task or with "a more effective use of the Christian forces in China in undertaking the task." The new day in China and the new urgency for a wise and powerful advance in the Christian permeation of Chinese life called for as large a degree of understanding and co-operation as the missionary forces could achieve.

In the critical portion of his study Rankin revealed an alertly discriminating mind and a staunch loyalty to principles—the marks of a true critic. This appears in his examination of the operation of the National Council and the dangers that confronted it.

The basis on which the Council was organized was that of voluntary co-operation, with full respect for the freedom and autonomy of the co-operating groups. The Council would have no authority over the programs of these groups and would have no separate missionary program of its own. Its functions would be advisory rather than directive. It was to be in no sense an ecclesiastical organization or a promoter of organic church union.

This basic principle, Rankin observed, soon became endangered. In its official actions the Council had been "commendably successful" in adhering to it. He wrote,

Nevertheless, because of the nature of its personnel and of a large part of its constituency, the Council is inevitably an influence for the promotion and development of a National Church. This is not to make any charge against the Council that it is overstepping the bounds of its constitution; it is simply to recognize that the influence of the Council is inevitably in the line of the sympathies and aims of the individuals which constitute it and of a considerable part of the constituency that supports it. Various individual members of the Council and of the staff are universally committed to organic unity and the development of a National Church in China, as is evidenced by their connections with the Church of Christ (recently organized) in China and by numerous utterances. A number of the organizations cooperating in the Council have entered the Church of Christ in China. Discussions in the annual meetings of the Council, while not dealing directly with organic unity, often express disapproval of the existing denominational divisions and a desire for a larger organic unity. These facts are cited simply to substantiate the statement that the Council is inevitably an influence for the promotion of the concept of a National Church. This concept is involved in any attempt to evaluate the place and importance of the Council (Thesis, p. 94 f.).

He examined the idea historically and in its meaning for the Christian movement in China. Out of his review of the development and character of the Roman Catholic Church and of the national churches in Europe, he reached several conclusions about organic unity: (1) that it has never brought about spiritual unity but rather by its authoritarian imposition of authority and forms has produced spiritual decline and disunity; (2) that its institutional emphasis has seldom developed a native and personal expression of Christianity; and (3) that it has often correlated and directed forces so as to exert a powerful force but not to the end of planting the gospel of Christ within the hearts of the people.

As to its meaning for the Christian movement in China, he pointed out that the concept of a national church was inconsistent with the central objectives of the National Council. Organic unity, according to history's record, would de-emphasize the importance of spiritual unity and make it more difficult to attain. Secondly, it would mean the abandonment of the principle of voluntary co-operation, which was the basic principle in the Council's organization. In a third place, as church instead of Council, it would tend to regard itself as "the church" and all who did not join it as outsiders only to be tolerated. It would thus become only another denomination making exclusive claims for itself. And, again, it would hinder rather than promote the aim of an indigenous Christianity in China. "Control, regulation, and direction" were inherent in its purpose. "If this were not so, there could be no sufficient reason for the organic relations," he said. To be truly indigenous Christianity must be free. Centralized control, whether national or foreign, cannot achieve it. A national church "under the direction and control of a comparatively small group of Chinese officials is only a little less opposed to the development of indigenous Christianity than a church controlled and directed by foreign missionaries" (Thesis, p. 107).

This Rankin regarded as the most serious danger for the future of what might become a most valuable instrument of missionary progress. By 1927 the advocates of organic union were promoting the idea on the ground of efficiency. Others were very conscious of the weakness of the Council and the dangers that beset it from within. Some of the latter were ready to isolate their groups altogether from the Council and its services; others, including Rankin, believed that some such co-operative organization was needed and that the Council was worth saving if it could be led to secure the permanence of its original character and aims. He wrote,

41

There is need for such an organization as the Council through which the separate organizations (denominational and other) can work at these tasks jointly. Each needs the experience and cooperation of the others in meeting the many questions and problems (of common concern) which arise. As an agency for erecting a spirit of sympathy and understanding, for cooperative effort and mutual help, for securing a Chinese viewpoint and approach to the work, for the gathering and making available of information on the Christian movement as a whole, the Council has a great service to render.

He was convinced, however, that the current trends of development were making it increasingly difficult for some denominational groups, such as the Southern Baptist missions, and the Chinese Leung Kwang Baptist Association, to cooperate. Either the trends must be arrested or these groups would be forced to go their separate ways entirely. The future of the Council was first of all the responsibility of the Council itself. In the conclusion of his thesis he set out in several principles what he deemed necessary for the Council to maintain its character and appeal as a co-operating body. These principles reveal some of his basic concepts in their relevance to the missionary enterprise:

1. If the Council is to be a safe organization for work in the Christian movement in China, it must recognize that it is primarily the individual (not Christians *en masse*) that "demands equality and repudiates the attitude of superiority" and that "the principle of free and autonomous" churches, not "Church" must be accepted.
2. There must be a recognition that Christian unity is not dependent upon organic unity.
3. There must be a fuller recognition that the Christian experience does not always express itself in the same forms.
4. It must be clearly recognized that those with similar expres-

兩廣浸信會神道學校第二十八屆畢業員生攝影一九三三年六月十六日

Some of the teachers and graduating class, Graves
Theological Seminary, Canton, China, 1933. Dr.
Rankin is at the left center of the back row.

Rankin Memorial Chapel, Fukuoka, Japan, 1954

sions and interpretations will naturally group themselves together; that they will desire to maintain an unhampered opportunity to deliver at its maximum the expression of the Christian experience which has been committed to them; and that to do this is not necessarily a violation of Christian unity. It is when this expression is taught as the only form of Christian experience that this unity is violated.

5. It must be more fully recognized that the only means of regulation, control and direction is the Holy Spirit. . . . There is a challenge here to the advocate of local, autonomous churches as well as to the advocate of organic unity. Neither denominational regulation and control nor the control of an organized unity can avail here. The Holy Spirit must be supreme in each individual, and each local church must be completely free under the power of the Holy Spirit to work out its own form of life.

These principles constituted not only a challenge to the Council, but to the various Christian groups, including Baptists, whose work would be vitally affected by its influence. On this point he was bold to express his own thought, although he was conscious that many in his group were in a mood to dissent:

If those who are strongly opposed to the principles of the National Church and who hold most strongly to the principles of individualism and local autonomy in the Christian experience, withhold all influence from the Council and leave it entirely to those who accept the principles of a National Church, the influence of the Council will quite inevitably be wholly for the development of the National Church. We do not mean to imply that one faction of opinion should enter the Council with the purpose of wresting the influence of the Council from another faction. In fact we have not observed that there has been any tendency in the Council to guard the control of the Council's influence. Through discussion and conference and through study and information the Council is forming opinions and conclusions in regard to Christian work. It is these opinions and conclusions which constitute the great influence of the Council. If a certain element of the Christian constituency in China considers that it has a principle that is vital and fundamental in the Christian experience, the possession of this principle constitutes a responsibility to give it a chance to exercise its true weight in the formation of the Council's opinions and conclusions. The constituency of each Christian organization in China will be greatly affected by the Council's influence whether or not some organizations have a part in shaping its influence. Too often the desire to guard one's own organization from harmful influence obscures the responsibility which that organization has in shaping the ideas which vitally concern its constituency. While the organization is being zealously guarded, the constituency for which the organization exists may be subjected to an influence which is considered vitally harmful, and which could have been largely averted had the organization not been so concerned with preserving itself from all evil contacts.

In short, the principles that led him to oppose corporate union led him to accept the responsibility of expressing those principles wherever possible.

As long as the Council provided an opportunity, as it did in 1928, he could see the value of co-operation with it. This was the spirit in which he faced the situation and in which he would return to the field:

We believe that as the spirit of such principles comes to exist more fully among the Christian organizations and workers in China, the Council will be able to render an increasingly valuable service to the whole Christian movement in China. On the other hand, we believe that to the extent in which this spirit does not exist the Council will become the agency of certain elements within the Christian movement and that its influence will be destructive to Christian unity and cooperation, and injurious otherwise to the building up of the Kingdom of God in China.

And to the eventuality he could not be irresponsibly indifferent.

The year in America thus meant a deeper grounding in essential Baptist principles, a clear perspective in relation to the missionary task and its problems, and, in addition, a fresh conviction of the importance of the interrelations of principle, purpose, and method. On the mission field as in the homeland, machinery (method) is easily over-magnified in consciousness and tends to assume the stature of principle. "We have never" easily advances to "we must not," and "we have always" to "we must." This crystallization of method Rankin held to be irrational. Methods are the instruments of purpose; purposes are the embodiment of principles. Principle is the determining factor—first principle, then purpose, then method.

Methods are subject to change to meet changing conditions. Changes in environmental conditions in China necessitated changes in some missionary methods and shifts here and there in points of emphasis also, for the sake of a more effective Christian impact upon the Chinese people. So long as changes remained true to principle they could be accepted on their merits in efficiency. But neither the strong grip of custom nor adventurous change for the sake of change must be determining factors in missionary policy. The governing factor is dynamic Christian principles and the purposes inherent in them. Nothing in method—oldness or newness, ease of operation or efficiency—must blind one to that.

Other fruits of the year came through a better acquaintance with the Southern Baptist constituency. He preached in many churches, taught in schools of missions, attended conventions and conferences, now observing through missionary eyes the spirit and program of the denomination. He could not fail to observe a recession from the high missionary enthusiasm of the Seventy-Five Million Campaign of the early 1920's, or the immense increase of expenditures for homeland projects. He was made to feel deeply that the conception of world missions was far short of the place it should hold in denominational consciousness.

On the other hand, the sympathetic hearing he received everywhere, the rising emphasis on evangelism and Christian education, the growth of the churches, and the reorganization of the administrative work of the Convention for more effective service, which was then in process—all gave to him a new appraisal of the spiritual and material resources of Southern Baptists. He was encouraged to believe that once they were aroused to what was taking place in the world and to the responsibility of Baptists to give their witness, they would respond.

The furlough, so rich for his own mind and heart, was rich also in what he gave. His quiet friendliness and sincere spirit in personal contacts left a warmth of pleasantness. The pastor of the church where he and his family chose to worship while in Louisville (if the writer may speak of himself a moment) was enriched in spirit, and his missionary interest and outlook received new and lasting proportions through frequent and informal contacts. From that day the two families were knit together in a fellowship no less than kinship. This was the kind of experience that came, if in less degree, to many in the homeland. In his public addresses a quiet power gave reality to the mission task and communicated his own feeling of urgency as he shared with Southern Baptists his understanding of the world situation and reminded them that the real measure of their greatness was the measure of their fellowship in the world mission of Jesus Christ.

IV
SEVEN TRYING YEARS
1928–35

The Rankins returned to Canton in the fall of 1928. At that time the political situation presented a more hopeful outlook. The government of Chiang Kai Shek was in power and gave promise of a more stable and reasonable rule. His successes against the Communists in the south had been followed by equally impressive victories as his armies marched northward. In 1928 he captured Nanking and made it the national capital, purposing to establish there a unified noncommunist government. In Canton there was comparative peace for a year or two, but the struggle for power was far from settled, and Communism was not dead. Its propaganda continued, and in 1931 the Chinese Communists were able again to take over the Canton government and plunge the area into war. The same year the Japanese began their invasion of China, first in the north (Manchuria) and later in Shanghai. Challenged by a foreign foe, the people of the nation rallied to Chiang Kai Shek, the military opposition of the Communists subsided, and Chiang was able to strengthen his government and establish a semblance of unity in a common cause. However, as soon as the challenge of Japan's sudden attack relaxed, the internal struggle for power started again.

The work of the missionaries could not escape the downdrag of the situation. The uncertainty and restlessness of the people, the increasing poverty and dislocation, changing laws, the increasing problems of Christian schools and churches, the fluctuating tides of antiforeign, anti-Christian feeling, plus the crippling effects of the world depression made the role of the missionary increasingly trying. This is reflected in the fact that between 1926 and 1933 the number of Protestant foreign missionary workers in the nation decreased by more than twenty-five hundred.

The missionaries of South China were troubled in heart and often discouraged, but patient and determined. Evangelists, teachers, doctors, and nurses carried on from day to day with outward calm. Reports to the Foreign Mission Board and the Southern Baptist Convention year after year, even in distressing times of declining resources from home and mounting local problems, never omitted the note of joy in the fruits of the gospel or the note of hope born of faith and of the long look. They were consciously about God's business, playing their several roles in the missionary drama with faith and steadfastness. And one cannot write the personal story of one of them without seeing the faces of others who labored with equal devotion and played an essential part in the work that he was able to do.

Theron Rankin's share of the load upon his return in 1928 was to continue his work as teacher and president of the Graves Theological Seminary. The year in America had given him new energy physically, intellectually, and spiritually. He had a broader horizon and deeper convictions concerning the task of missions. Thumping beneath his usually calm and deliberate manner was a fresh enthusiasm for the work of preparing Chinese young men to preach and teach the gospel. The story of his devotion to the work of the seminary is one that honors its history and testifies to his evaluation of the worth of theological education in the Christian world task. It is also a story of hardship, tensions, and persistent hope in a rapidly changing pattern of events.

The seminary had a humble beginning. Before 1870 Dr. R. H. Graves organized classes for inquirers and believers. By 1870 there were a few young men who were preparing for the preaching ministry, and the instruction was fitted to them. Until 1890 Dr. Graves was the only teacher, the classes meeting in a room in the Graves home. In 1890 they were moved to a room in a new chapel. In 1891 Dr. G. W. Greene, Mrs. Rankin's father, a teacher at Wake Forest College in North Carolina, was appointed to join Dr. Graves and until his death was a strong force in the work of the mission. In 1907 the school was moved to new and ample quarters in the Tungshan area of Canton, which was to become a shining center of Baptist work. In 1905, which marked the fiftieth anniversary of Dr. Graves' missionary service, the Foreign Mission Board had appropriated five thousand dollars for the new building, and the seminary was given its name in his honor.

By 1923, when Rankin was added to the teaching staff, the seminary was approaching its peak. Dr. P. H. Anderson was then president. In 1922 there were sixty students; in 1923, seventy-five; in 1924, seventy-nine. But this progress was to be short-lived. The national upheaval was having disturbing effects upon the work of missions, particularly education. The seminary was not untouched. In 1925 Dr. Anderson resigned as president and, as stated, Rankin was asked to take his place at the helm. It fell to him to pilot the ship through the stormy seas ahead.

At first he had as colleagues two able missionary teachers, W. D. King and G. W. Greene, Jr., and two or three Chinese

49

teachers. But the intellectual and social ferment of the revolution was at work. The number of students declined, and in 1926 and 1927 it was reduced to fifty. The next year the Rankins were in America on a much-needed furlough, Mr. King serving as president meanwhile. The current did not change. When Dr. Rankin, having won his degree in Louisville, returned, he found the same spirit of criticism and restlessness among the students; there were also mounting difficulties from without. But, refreshed in spirit and with a strong faculty, he set about his work with renewed hope for the future.

Then came the "upset." In the fall of 1929 the financial debacle in America plunged the Foreign Mission Board into a crisis that could mean nothing but retrenchment in its whole mission program. Already the appropriations for the seminary had declined; the president found himself in a "slough of despond." He began to think of himself and what was happening to him. The bigness of the task, the opposing forces, the mounting difficulties on one hand and on the other the smallness and weakness of what he was trying to do—these were almost too much for him. The last problem was magnified by what he had seen in America—the seminaries with many hundreds of students, the large and prosperous churches, the successes and prominence of his former fellow students. As he disclosed later, he found himself making comparison between these and his position and wondering whether he might not have done better at home. Years later, recalling his state of mind, he said, "At the end of eight years on the mission field it seemed to me that everything was a complete failure. . . . We felt it would be better to close the Seminary. . . . I was discouraged to the bottom."

A man of his faith and depth of religious experience could not dwell long under a juniper tree. Of his inward struggle he said, "Always deep down inside a voice would speak and say, 'Quit kidding yourself. You know in your heart that you came here because you could not have done anything else and have been honest with your Lord. And it makes no difference how much of a failure your life may seem to be. . . . You know what the Lord wants you to do. Go on and do it!' " And that is what he did, to the glory of God. As has happened so many times with the servants of God, the valley led to a higher and more secure spiritual level. He gained a decisive victory over himself at a point of conflict that others were not aware of. Never afterward did he let what might happen to him become a chief concern. His one business was to serve Christ in the advancement of his kingdom. He was content to leave personal success or failure in the hands of God.

This did not mean that his task would be easier. Harder times and baffling problems were yet to come. In 1931 Mr. King resigned as teacher to enter another type of work which he felt would be more fruitful. This was a serious blow to the seminary and shocked and puzzled the president, since it left the seminary in serious straits. He wrote to Dr. Ray, the secretary of the Foreign Mission Board, "With Mr. King's resignation we are now short three teachers. We absolutely must have two. It is next to impossible to secure teachers who are able to meet the requirements of seminary work. This is even more difficult now than it was some years ago, because the preachers of the old type of Chinese training and education are not at all acceptable to the present-day generation of students." This he knew because only recently the students had protested to the board of trustees against the election of a Chinese teacher because, they said, "His training is not high enough." Reduced student body, reduced budget, and now a reduced missionary faculty! The task was like that of a man trying to mount a descending escalator. However, in the fall the president announced with a note of hope that all classes would open, that a "very fine man" had agreed to begin teaching in January, and that two others were in prospect for the following year. "I trust," he wrote, "that by another year we shall have a first-rate faculty at the Seminary."

Meanwhile, the financial condition of the Foreign Mission Board was growing more desperate, affecting the entire program of the mission. The strong current of contributions for missions in the early twenties had shrunk to a sluggish, dwindling stream. Missionaries on furlough had little prospect of returning. Any hope of a new appointee to teach at the seminary had to be abandoned. The school had to depend more and more upon Chinese teachers and Chinese money for its life, and at best in the circumstances of the time that was not a very promising outlook.

The situation was made more poignant in 1932 by the loss of the other missionary teacher, G. W. Greene, also the treasurer of the mission. His account books, his correspondence with the Board, his close connection with the work in the various stations, and his understanding of the world situation convinced him that further retrenchments were inevitable. In his judgment, it would be better to reduce the number of missionaries than to leave off the support of national evangelists and fieldworkers. He also felt that he, a layman, could be spared more easily than an ordained, theologically trained missionary. Of Dr. Rankin's reaction to his decision Mr. Greene writes, "Theron urged me, not unduly, not to leave. He was a leader of men who did not feel that he had to make their decisions for them. He stressed the view that each person could and should get his orders from above." Accepting this loss, as that of Mr. King the year before, as graciously as he could, Dr. Rankin could not conceal his distress and discouragement.

What could be done? Facing what appeared to be a dead end, he raised the question whether he, a missionary of the Board, should resign and put the responsibility of finding a way out squarely on the local board of trustees. He frankly said he did not want to resign and had no thought but to remain as teacher and "do our utmost to carry on right where we are." He was not trying to save himself by getting "out from under," but to save the seminary. He was almost apologetic for writing about his problem: "Let me assure you that while we are struggling with our own problems we are not unmindful of the great problems you have to deal with. . . . I am simply saying to you what we are compelled to say to ourselves, with the thought that perhaps you can give us some light."

Dr. Ray replied with sympathetic and bracing wisdom. His counsel was that Dr. Rankin should by no means risk the complete dissolution of the seminary which might follow his resignation. Suspension for a year might be necessary, but "hold everything as an organization intact. . . . It may be that this is a very good time to show the Chinese their responsibility towards it. We, of course, will not lose our ideal and our appreciation of the valuable work that institution can do."

Enheartened by this point of view, Dr. Rankin remained at the helm to do two things: (1) keep the school open, and (2) find the best way to enlist full Chinese support. The first he was able to do by limiting the number of classes offered and using volunteer teachers from other schools. The second would require a facing of basic facts and principles by both the Chinese and the mission, matters involving the functions of the missionary organization and Chinese Baptists and problems of co-operation and authority, upon which there was not entire unanimity at the time.

In the early years of the seminary it had been financed and controlled by the Foreign Mission Board. Even after the Chinese Baptist constituency had organized the Leung Kwang Association and had many institutions of its own, theological education remained entirely under foreign control. Until the revolution of 1912 or 1914 no serious question was raised, although the seminary, as trainer of pastors and leaders, was the key institution in the progress of the churches. After that, however, both the growth of the seminary and the growing self-consciousness of the Chinese people made it necessary that the Chinese should have a more intimate relation to its work. The Board hoped to accomplish this by including Chinese representatives on the board of trustees. This new board, however, still had to refer all matters of personnel, budget, and policy to the Foreign Mission Board for approval. In the thought of the Chinese it remained essentially a "foreign institution" and, although they appreciated what was being done for them and co-operated sincerely, they could not promote it effectively among the people as their responsibility. Consequently, when the crisis came, the Chinese Baptists were slow to respond.

Let it be said here that the only reason that the seminary had remained a mission-controlled institution was a feeling that because of their limitations in resources and theological leadership the Chinese were not ready to assume full responsibility. The South China Mission favored the principle of indigenous Christianity as entirely congenial with Baptist faith and purpose. The early missionaries, for example, established a girls' school in order to stimulate the Chinese to establish a boys' school which would be solely their responsibility. They promoted the organization of the Leung Kwang Baptist Association as an autonomous body. The churches were developed to become self-directing, self-propagating, and self-supporting, as free as Baptist churches in America. So the present problem was not one of principle but one of finding a basis of operation that would win the full support of Chinese Baptists and insure the life of the seminary.

On their part, the Chinese leaders were not ready to ask that ownership be transferred to the association. They did not wish to press the indigenous principle that far. The most pressing thing was to keep the school alive. Pursuant to that, the Leung Kwang Association in 1931 proposed a new policy which, it was thought, would command a saving support. They proposed that the seminary board of trustees, composed of both missionaries and Chinese representatives, be empowered to conduct the school without having to refer matters of personnel, budget, administration, etc., to the Foreign Mission Board in America; a committee was appointed to confer with the executive committee of the mission. It was a policy of joint responsibility at the local level.

On its part, the executive committee of the mission felt that full responsibility would be the best guarantee of full support. Dr. Rankin, who was a member of the committee, proposed that "the Mission discontinue operating the Graves Theological Seminary not later than the close of the

school year 1933, and that we state to the Leung Kwang Association that in case they wish to conduct such a school we
are prepared to assist them in the teaching staff and finan-
cially, the extent of such help to be determined on the basis
of the plans made by the Association."

Dr. Rankin summed up the meaning of this as follows:

Heretofore the Mission has been conducting the Seminary and
the Chinese Association has been helping in *our* work. We think
the time has come when the status should be reversed, so that the
Chinese Association will be conducting the Seminary and the
Mission will be helping in *their* work. . . . Under the plan we
are not asking the Association to take over something which we
think they ought to do. We simply say to them, that if they consider they ought to undertake this work when we discontinue doing it, we stand ready to assist them. They are not tied to any
plans; they can make their own and project their program as they
think best.

He heartily supported this plan for three reasons: (1) It
would make theological education an integral part of the
life and work of the Chinese Baptist Association; (2) it
would eliminate the problems and hazards of joint control;
(3) it was a step forward in giving to the Baptist work an
indigenous character. "The Mission has carried this responsibility for sixty years; the Chinese are capable of taking it
up, and it ought by all means to be on them and not on
the Mission."

Although some in the mission and in the Foreign Board
thought it was too radical, after some delay it was approved
by both bodies. The Chinese association was fearful for its
ability to carry such a load, but recognizing its primary responsibility, accepted it at its meeting in October, 1933,
and appointed a board of trustees to begin plans for taking

over the school. Dr. Rankin, of course, resigned as president while continuing as teacher, but he was urged to remain in charge until a suitable Chinese person could be found. This he consented to do for the school year of 1933–1934.

The task now was to help the Chinese Baptists save *their* school. In March, 1934, he wrote to Dr. C. E. Maddry, who had become executive secretary of the Foreign Mission Board in 1933, pleading for help as he had never done before. The effort of the Chinese to keep the school open was falling short. He wrote,

> In one sense I might say that this responsibility is not ours now, since the school has been turned over to the Chinese; but this will not obviate the fact that unless some way is found to help this Seminary in its present crisis the Baptist work in South China will suffer greatly in the years to come. . . . The Chinese brethren are earnestly seeking to carry the load put on them, but I don't see how they can carry it all as yet. Increased help from the Foreign Mission Board, I think, is imperative to save the school from collapse. I feel it within me to make an urgent appeal to save us from such a calamity because of the personal distress of having the Seminary fail under my administration; but this is a small matter as compared with the loss of the school to the service of the Kingdom of God in China.

His "urgent appeal" was for $300 for the current year and a promise of $600 for 1935. On the day that he received the letter Dr. Maddry replied,

> In the same mail I received a special gift from a lady for $500.-00 to be used on the foreign field in any way I might determine. . . . I am sending you in this letter a special letter of credit for $300.00. . . . Also I am going to include in the budget for 1935 the $600.00 requested. . . . Also I am going to be on the lookout for a new missionary to give himself wholly to assist-

ing the Chinese brethren in the work of the Seminary. . . .
With the help of God we are not going to retreat any further.

By that letter the darkness was turned to dawning and the
dawning to noonday fair!

The school was saved. After the opening of the first session under the new administration (fall of 1934), Dr. Rankin was able to write:

The session thus far has been the most encouraging one since I
have been connected with the school. The Chinese leaders have
taken hold with a determination and spirit of consecration which
leads me to believe that the Seminary is now planted on a foundation which will not give way. . . . When I last wrote I was
exceedingly discouraged about the future of the school; now I am
more encouraged than I have been at any time since I became
connected with it.

Thus it was given to him to end his twelve years with the
seminary on a high and hopeful note. Before the end of the
next session he was called to other responsibilities.

In January, 1932, the Board asked Dr. Rankin to accept
the added responsibilities of treasurer of the mission. He
had served temporarily in the office in 1925–1926 while Mr.
Greene was on furlough and brought to it his experience as
a bookkeeper in his earlier years. The routines of the new
work were therefore familiar to him.

But keeping accounts, receiving, and disbursing were
only incidental to the real business of the treasurer in those
days. The big words were Decline, Debt, Retrenchment; the
big task, Survival. After the financial crisis of 1929 the Foreign Mission Board was unable to reduce its program on the
mission fields fast enough to keep within the limits of the

rapidly declining contributions. Consequently, its indebtedness mounted. There were budget cuts in 1930 and 1931. In 1932 by order of the Convention the appropriations were 12 per cent less than in 1931, calling for a further severe cut in 1933. In these circumstances the duties and burdens of the treasurer were greatly increased.

The Board expected him to lead in working out with the mission the necessary reductions of budgets, which entailed a re-evaluation of various projects, redistribution of responsibilities, the abandonment here and there of work that was very precious to those engaged in it, and with all of this, the preservation of a morale that would hold all to the common task. The treasurer, together with the executive committee of the mission, was the mediator between the mission and the Board. There was constant correspondence with the Board about matters ranging from small adjustments in a missionary's salary to the collapse of a missionary house in Wuchow.

A part of the retrenchment was the sale of land which the Board in better times had purchased for future use. The treasurer had a central place in the sales, in legal matters involved, and in the collection and transmission of land money to the Board with full account of all transactions. This one matter took much time and patience. Sometimes the Board's title to pieces of property had to be cleared up. The Chinese raised the question of the moral right of the Board to sell at the high current price land for which it had paid little. The Chinese Baptists were opposed to selling on the market land which they would need for the expansion of Christian institutions and to sending the proceeds to America.

One may be sure that this immersion in business was not

in the missionary's early dream. Although neither he nor his fellow missionaries had envisaged the experiences of this trying time, they were able to keep their eyes and hearts free to see the goodness of God and reap blessings from their difficulties. In July, 1932, Dr. Rankin, reporting the meeting of the mission, wrote:

In spite of the conditions we are facing, this meeting was the most hopeful I have attended in several years. I think we are being forced to learn that even though we do not have much money and much of the regular work we have been doing is being forced to close, still we can find large opportunities for giving the gospel to the people. Of course we are greatly concerned about the future of the Board, but I think we are learning not to be so completely dependent on money.

What he was experiencing in the seminary and as treasurer all the missionaries were experiencing in their respective tasks. Yet they did not give up; they became inured to hardship and sacrifice. The present situation was only an intensification of the circumstances that much earlier had caused an older missionary to say to a newcomer, "If you ever need something you don't have and can't get, just come to me and I'll show you how to do without it."

The story of these seven trying years must include reference to Dr. Rankin's part in some matters only indirectly related to his work in the seminary and as treasurer.

An example is the problem that arose with reference to the girls' school in Canton (Pooi To). In the 1920's the government set up a new educational program under the control of a central governmental authority. All schools engaged in general education were required to register, to observe prescribed ceremonials honoring Sun Yat-sen, and to accept governmental regulations, including limitations on religious instruction. Throughout China this raised serious problems for education under Christian auspices. For Chinese Christian organizations and for missionary organizations alike, central governmental control of Christian schools raised fundamental questions of rights. The religious significance of the ceremonial was variously interpreted—to many it was worship; to many others it was simply a patriotic salute. The limitations of religious instruction contradicted the central purpose of Christian education. The whole structure of the Christian program was at stake. The alternative was to register the schools and accept the controls or to be outlawed and closed.

In Canton two schools faced the issue, Pui Ching (the boys' school) and Pooi To (the girls' school). Pui Ching was owned and operated by Chinese Baptists. Although the constituency was far from unanimous, the trustees decided to register the school, accepting the form if not the spirit and purpose of the government's regulations. Their feeling was that to abandon education as a part of the Christian program would be disastrous; also, that the present situation was temporary. They did not believe that under Chiang Kai-shek, the rising leader, any radical anti-Christian movement would develop, and they were hopeful that the regulations could be changed to give greater freedom to the Christian schools.

There was a different situation in the case of the girls' school. It was the property of the Foreign Mission Board, operated by a board of trustees who were responsible to it. The question of registration was not a matter to be settled by the local board without the approval of the Foreign Mission Board. It involved missionary and American opinion

61

and the policy of the Board, and to submit to governmental control of education that reached into the curriculum and life within the school was foreign to their way of thinking. The schools of the mission could not become the instruments of the Chinese government, even formally.

In the spring of 1930 some decision had to be made. The trustees were unwilling to accept either horn of the dilemma —register or close—or to defy the order. They agreed on another course which would free the Board from the necessity of decision and permit the Chinese Baptists to choose their own course. Through Dr. Rankin, who was one of the trustees, they sought the judgment of the Board before taking action, but due to the absence of Secretary Ray in South America they were unable to obtain it. In that situation they passed the following resolutions, hoping the Board would approve later. They planned to recommend to the Board: (1) that they turn the school over to the Leung Kwang Baptist Association, thus placing the responsibility for its policy upon the Chinese; (2) that, pending final transfer, the present organization be kept intact by the Board for one year; and (3) that the Board continue for the present the support which they had been giving to the school, this as an assurance of sympathy and support as the Chinese sought to save their Christian schools and secure greater freedom of operation.

Dr. Rankin, in reporting the action to the Board, said little about his personal views, but a fellow missionary and close friend interpreted them as follows:

He was not opposed to registration of the schools simply as registration. He was opposed to registration as it was being imposed at the time with the hampering regulations and regimentation.

62

At the same time he was still more opposed to the view that the Mission should be preemptory and refuse to consider the best judgment of Cantonese Baptists even when one is not prepared to go along with them in all their conclusions. For him, the decision, in the last analysis, needed to be left to them for the good of the cause of the Kingdom, and he displayed a great trust in them to do what was best under the leadership of the Holy Spirit even when he himself might not agree with them in the entirety of their thinking. It was his view that they should be enabled to make their own decisions with regard to matters which seemed to him to have passed beyond the place where he or any other westerner could control satisfactorily. It was not an easy decision to reach, but he so concluded.

He gave much thought to the problems of missions in relation to the government of the country and came to the conclusion that if they considered education an essential part of their task, Christians might consent to work within the limitations imposed by the government and not demand ideal conditions. The business of Christianity is to prove itself and win its way, rather than make its work contingent upon favorable attitudes. He had great respect for Paul's attitude expressed in the thirteenth chapter of Romans.

Another conviction voiced in the recommendation to the Board was the right of Chinese Baptists to make their own choices in the working out of their denominational life; they should not be considered as wards of American Baptists. Doubtless they would make mistakes. Many times Dr. Rankin was heard to say, "I am afraid they will make as many and as great mistakes as we have made, but they have the same freedom to make them as we have claimed for ourselves." He had a great respect for the faith, intelligence, and consecration of Chinese Baptists.

Still another conviction behind the action was that Baptist brotherhood should not be conditioned on uniformity in judgment or conformity in practice. Even though the Chinese were willing to register the school and choose methods not after our patterns, they deserved our continued support as our brothers in the Baptist faith.

In writing to the Board he apologized for himself and the other missionary trustees for agreeing to the action without previous approval by the Board, and added, "I am sure there will be some criticisms of our having done this, both here and probably on the part of the Board, but we simply could do nothing else. . . . Of course we are hoping very much that the Foreign Mission Board will be able to approve of the action which we have taken for this one year. However, those of us who had a part in taking the action are prepared to accept whatever results may be involved in our having taken this step." Happily it was approved, the government regulations were eased, the school enjoyed large liberty, and by 1935 the Board was in process of giving it a deed for the land on which it stood.

These seven trying years were not all conflict and shadow. Alongside such matters as have been presented there were many experiences that were springs of joy and refreshment of spirit. We have heard much of the power of the evangelical witness of the missionary home in pagan lands; we must not omit its meaning to the missionaries themselves. A person who visits the foreign fields comes away thankful for the Foreign Mission Board's provision, wherever possible, of comfortable houses for the missionaries. They remind him of calm harbors in which one finds rest from the sea and fresh supplies for body and spirit. The home of the Rankins was such a place. The house itself had a look of calmness and comfort. And the spirit of life within made it a place where tensions could be relaxed and energies and courage restored.

In their home the Rankins found much joy. In 1929, as if heaven were undergirding them for the hard years ahead, an angel visited them—and stayed. They named her Mary Lee. Page was then six years old. Whatever they did to the quietness of the haven, those two kept the springs of happiness open and chased away many a shadow. They kept laughter and play alive when trouble frowned.

There was room, however, for much reading and thought. Dr. Rankin's early-formed reading habit was thwarted often, but not broken, by the exactions of many duties. It was the horizons, insights, and information of well-chosen books that helped him keep his head above water and clear his eyes to what was transpiring in the world. His book orders included not only practical books for his preaching but also more solid books of permanent value. He always kept a prophetic book at hand. Thus he kept his mental outlook abreast with his practical experience. This meant constant re-enforcement.

In addition, the Rankin home was a spiritual retreat for the renewal of faith. In meditation and prayer the problems of the day and the concerns for tomorrow were brought into better perspective and presented before God. Mrs. Rankin once remarked that she first learned about many things that were on her husband's mind as he spoke to God about them in his prayers. It was his comfort that hers was a congenial spirit and that together they could bare their needs to God and find his guidance.

There were also the heartening social pleasures of contacts with other Christian families. The exchange and mingling of experience not only nurtured a bracing community consciousness but often broke the tensions of the day by the discovery that there was something to laugh about; it kept alive a saving sense of humor, "without which," to quote Dr. Rankin, "a missionary could not live."

In the work itself there were at every stage experiences that spoke of the fruits of the gospel and renewed the joys of serving Christ. Were it not for glimpses here and there of spiritual passion and the triumphs of the gospel in the hearts of men, a person reading the voluminous correspondence—most of it strictly business—might get the impression that the framework of missions was the major concern. Doors are opened upon the brighter side of experience by paragraphs in business letters like this: "In spite of reductions in funds, lack of missionaries, etc., the work in Canton is progressing in a most encouraging way. On yesterday over eighty people were baptized in three of our city churches." Not only in Canton but in every part of the mission the spirit of evangelism and the manifest power of Christ proved the worthwhileness of the work and strengthened hearts to go on with joy and thanksgiving.

The report of a service of worship is a high example of how the fellowship in the churches was a fountain of rich resources. It was about an Easter service in the Tungshan church:

It has been raining most of the day. The sky was dark and overcast in the morning and later developed into a slow, drizzly rain. And yet it has been a day of sunshine in God's vineyard, glorious sunshine.

At eight o'clock this morning the Christian people of Canton gathered on the grounds of the Graves Seminary to hold a united service in commemoration of the resurrection of Jesus. More than three thousand people came from all parts of the city; old and young, students and coolies, rich and poor, a great host came together to commemorate the Risen Lord. If you could have stood where I stood, on the top terrace, and looked down on that throng of Chinese people worshipping our Living Lord, you too would have seen the sunshine through the rain.

At ten thirty our Tungshan Sunday school service began. We have a department which is conducted in English for English speaking Chinese who have come back from abroad, with about one hundred and fifty members. The service this morning was *all* sunshine; there were no shadows anywhere as ten of these young people, who had been examined by the church on Saturday afternoon, were accepted for baptism. Some of us had sat with them when they were examined and heard them give their testimonies of their love for Christ and their faith in him. No amount of rain could shut out the sunshine of that experience. [A large group of these American-born Chinese young people regularly met in the Rankin home on Sunday evenings for a religious program and social fellowship.]

Then came the morning church service. By that time it was raining hard, but fully twelve hundred people came through the rain to feel the warmth of God's sunshine in that service. What a commemoration of our Lord's resurrection it was! The congregation in itself was a tremendous testimony to the power of the Risen Christ—more than twelve hundred people, probably ninety percent of them Christians, in a city where only fifty years ago not more than two or three hundred Christians could have been found in any congregation. The opening period of silent worship, the beautiful music, the Scripture lesson and prayer, all prepared us for the simple earnest message from the pastor. Our hearts were filled full as we saw twenty-nine portray through baptism their own death and resurrection in our Lord. A father and mother and their boy of ten years; boys and girls from the schools; an elderly man who, after having been refused baptism for two years because he retained his concubine, had made provisions for her to leave him, and had come back to ask again to be received—these all came down into the water, were buried, were raised, and went out to walk in newness of life.

After the baptism "the light of the knowledge of the glory of God in the face of Jesus Christ" shone full upon us "in the breaking of the bread." There were about nine hundred who in the quietness of that moment ate of the bread and drank of the cup to commemorate what our Lord has done for us in his death. The service was finished and we walked out into the rain. But it wasn't raining in God's vineyard; it was all sunshine there.

Other letters tell of evangelistic services and Bible conferences in schools and churches, in which "many thousands of people heard the gospel preached and the Scriptures taught . . . and many church members found more joy in their faith."

I went to Shiuchow [1934] while their Workers' Bible Conference was being held, and came away with such a good *feeling* about the work there. [Shiuchow was the home of D:. Rankin's brother, Manley W. Rankin, who became a missionary in 1924 and since then has been one of our most faithful and effective missionaries, engaged principally in rural evangelism among the Hakka-speaking people.] During the past several years I have made trips there and often come away feeling depressed. The Shiuchow work suffered tremendously during the disturbances of several years ago and by the reduction of funds. The property was occupied by soldiers; the missionaries were forced to leave and were not able to live on the station for several years, and when some of them were able to return, they had to live in small native houses which were terribly hot and uncomfortable; [native] workers were cut off and schools closed; and finally, as through sheer sympathy in the load which the workers were trying to carry, the church building itself fell down.

But the sunshine is always behind the clouds. Some of the missionaries are already back on the field, laboring to build things up again. The women of Virginia sent $5000.00 to rebuild the church; the missionaries and Chinese Christians gave of their own funds and sought contributions from other sources; the Mission found a plan for remodeling a school building to serve as residences for two missionaries. When I went this time I saw the light breaking through the shadows. Ten or twelve preachers and evangelists from the country round about were there in conference seeking for more of the power of the gospel in their lives and for more effective ways of building up God's work in China. The needs of that field are still great and the shadows still hang about, but the light of God's blessings shines through.

The financial crisis began to ease in 1933. Secretary Ray and the Foreign Mission Board had carried on since 1929 with rare ability. They had saved the missionary program of Southern Baptists. At the beginning of 1933 Dr. Charles E. Maddry became executive secretary, with Dr. Ray as his associate. This gave to Dr. Ray a much-deserved relief and brought to the work a man of proven administrative ability. For a number of years Dr. Maddry had served as secretary of Baptist work in North Carolina and as promotional secretary in the Southern Baptist Convention. He already had won the esteem of the denomination, not only by his ability, but by his spirit. He was much more than a business executive; he had the vision of a prophet and the heart of an evangelist. He was a man of great compassion who felt the trials through which the missionaries were passing. Moreover, he was thoroughly committed to world missions and brought to his task strong determination and unusually strong persuasive power.

It was in March, 1934, that he wrote to Dr. Rankin, "With the help of God we are not going to retreat any further." Around the world a new day was dawning for Southern Baptist missions.

In January, 1935, Dr. Maddry visited Canton where for the first time he and Dr. Rankin met. It was a major experience for both of them, especially Dr. Rankin. For him it was a turning point in his ministry, summoning him to a new field, new tasks, and greater responsibilities.

V

SECRETARY FOR THE ORIENT
1935–39

Few men in Southern Baptist history have undertaken a
more difficult task than Dr. Maddry did when in 1933 he
accepted the executive secretaryship of the Foreign Mission
Board. The financial depression had reduced its resources to
an almost unbearable limit. At home the staff was at little
more than stand-by strength. Abroad in sixteen countries its
work was depleted and lacking in cohesiveness and co-ordina-
tion. For example, in China the four missions were entirely
independent of one another; in the separate missions individual action, without seeking the judgment of the mission,
frequently overlooked the needs of the work as a whole. The
secretary's desk was piled with letters about matters that
should have been attended to locally. In addition to financial
recovery, he faced the task of the reorganization of the staff
and administrative procedures at home and abroad. And this
he did so wisely and thoroughly that no change was needed
when he retired from office.

Happily, within a year the financial situation began to
improve, definite steps were taken to reduce the debt, credit
with the banks was assured, and the denomination began to
rally to an aggressive program.

Central in Dr. Maddry's plans for reorganization was the
appointment of three regional secretaries of the Board—one
to serve the Orient, one Europe, Africa, and the Near East,

one Latin America. One of the purposes of his visit to the Orient in 1935 was to find a suitable man for that area. He knew that much would depend upon the first man chosen for the new venture, for such an office might easily become more disruptive than helpful. Among the missionaries there was considerable skepticism about the wisdom of it.

The choice fell upon Dr. Rankin. Although they had not met face to face, an extensive correspondence over a period of two years had acquainted Dr. Maddry with Dr. Rankin's ability as an administrator and with some of his attitudes and insights in matters of policy. These impressions and what he had heard friends and fellow missionaries say evidently had given him a mental picture of a man of stature, for when they met, Dr. Maddry's first remark was, "You are not as big a man as I expected to see." Two days afterward he cabled the Board his nomination of Dr. Rankin as secretary for the Orient. Years later he wrote in his autobiography, "I felt then, and I know now, that this was the greatest thing I ever did for foreign missions."

To accept the assignment was no easy decision for Dr. Rankin. It meant giving up the work that for fourteen years had claimed his energies and devotion, just when the work seemed to have reached the highroad of progress. The roots of his devotion to the missionaries, the people, and the work in South China were deep. Moreover, his contacts with the Chinese, which had kept his work so personal in its objectives, would be decreased. He saw the new assignment as a promotion only to a harder task and increased responsibilities, to a rather hazardous experience, and to a separation from direct personal missionary service. He accepted it, therefore, not as a personal preference, but as a summons to what he saw to be a needed service. Faced by the challenge to

71

follow his expressed concept of true Christian living as "individuality in community" and of self-denying teamwork as necessary to effective advance, he could do nothing else. He would give what he would ask of others in the common undertaking—one's best effort toward missionary advance.

In the weeks following, as they traveled together, both he and Dr. Maddry were heartened by the attitudes of the missionaries. One missionary remarked, "I don't like the idea of a boss, but if we must have one, I would rather have Theron than any other." Another (a veteran who felt it would be difficult for many to adjust to the new order) said that in his judgment Theron Rankin was the best man in China for the job. Everywhere they went hope was strengthened of receiving the confidence and support of the missionaries in the new venture. With this support they could build a stronger foundation for the work of the new office.

It was a happy coincidence that the new assignment came as the Rankins were finishing their second term on the field and were scheduled to spend the year 1935–1936 in America. In Richmond Dr. Rankin had the opportunity of studying the entire setup of the board, of becoming personally acquainted with the staff and the members, and of talking over leisurely with them and Dr. Maddry the duties of his new office. Through his addresses and articles for the Baptist papers he did much to inform the denomination of the situation in the Orient and press the necessity of supporting the expanding program. Dr. Maddry requested him to write an article explaining to our Baptist people—some of whom questioned the need of it—the purpose and function of the regional secretary. A few paragraphs from that article will reveal how thoroughly and in what spirit he had envisaged the work that was before him:

It will be the responsibility of this Secretary to act as the Foreign Mission Board's representative on the field. The relationship of the Board to the missionaries on the field is in no sense that of an employer to employees. Neither can the relationship of the Secretary for the Orient to the missionaries be that of one who is set over them to exercise authority. The fact is fully recognized, however, by all who are concerned in our missionary work that there are certain responsibilities and duties in the work of the missions which the Foreign Mission Board must assume directly.

The Secretary for the Orient will serve as a connecting link between the Board and the Missions. It will be his duty to keep in intimate touch with the work in all of the Missions through travel and personal visits, and to keep the Board in contact with the needs and conditions of the work as a whole. He will represent the Board in conferences with each mission in the preparation of the budget of the missions and in matters connected with the Board's property. He will give his assistance to the missions in their efforts to achieve a greater amount of unity and cooperation in their programs of work. Conditions which arose from the lack of funds and new missionaries during the past years have produced a considerable amount of individual and uncorrelated work. The missionaries have realized so fully the need to re-establish the cooperative programs of work that each of the missions has asked the Foreign Mission Board to approve a set of resolutions drawn up by themselves, which, it is hoped, will accomplish this purpose.

This secretary will seek to become also a connecting link between the Board and the individual work of his fellow-missionaries. In order to do this he will endeavor to spend a part of his time with individual missionaries in the work they are doing, trying to share with them their problems and needs, and to see their tasks as they see them. He will hope to be used as a medium for the exchange of ideas and methods of work as he goes from place to place. He will work also to keep the Board in intimate touch with these individual conditions.

The missionaries on the field believe that not only should those within each Mission work together in a cooperative program in order to accomplish the best results; they believe also that the various Missions should work toward a common end, having as much coordination and unity of effort and work as possible. They believe this is especially true of the four Missions in China. Without some one to act as a medium for unifying the work and objectives of these Missions they can easily develop into separate and individualistic units which have little in common. The Secretary for the Orient will be expected to serve the Missions in working for this end. There are several undertakings which call immediately for the joint efforts of all our Baptist forces in China, both missionaries and Chinese.

The task which will underlie all other responsibilities is that of being a missionary with his fellow-missionaries in Japan and China. If he cannot fulfil these other duties, and at the same time continue to be a missionary serving with missionaries, he will have failed in the greatest essential.

After establishing headquarters in Shanghai and finding a home for his family there in the summer of 1936, the new secretary's first undertaking was to get firsthand knowledge of conditions and needs and to establish mutual understanding and sympathetic relations in the various missions. According to Mrs. Rankin, his first year he was at home only once for as long as three weeks together. After a period in the Central China Mission, contiguous to Shanghai, he went in October to Canton for the celebration of the centennial of Baptist work in China. This was a very important experience for a comprehensive view of the historical picture and insight into the contemporary situation. There were present missionaries and Chinese Baptist leaders from every part of China and distinguished visitors from abroad.

A central feature of the program was a series of addresses in which missionaries reviewed various phases of the history and Chinese representatives spoke about the future. Dr. Rankin was deeply impressed as the story of the Baptist witness in China was unfolded, and especially by the Chinese leaders as they spoke out of deep faith and insight, avowing with confidence the purpose of Chinese Baptists under the leadership of the Holy Spirit to take upon themselves the burden of giving the gospel of redemption to the people of China. To him they were the prophets of a new and greater era of Christianity in China.

As he proceeded into other parts of China and Japan, he perceived the centennial to be truly representative of what was everywhere present. There was agreement that the historic elements of mission service found in our Lord's own ministry must remain central: evangelistic witness, education for Christian life and leadership, and a Christian ministry of love to the physical and social needs of men. There were only differences in emphasis, different evaluations, here and there.

Another fact that could not be missed at the centennial was the growing strength of Chinese churches and leaders. Here the fruits of history were tremendous. Baptist churches everywhere were multiplying and assuming increasing responsibility for their own maintenance and program. Conventions of Baptist churches were alive and aggressive in their sense of mission. In the four Chinese missions this was true. It was true also in Japan. There the missionaries had worked out a plan by which the West Japan Baptist Convention would share closely in the program of the mission. All policies and projects, even the sending of new missionaries, would be determined in consultation with the executive council of the convention. In conferences with the missionaries and Japanese leaders Dr. Rankin noted how freely and thoroughly various aspects of the program were discussed. He wrote, "As we listened and noted the consecration, intelligence and ability of the discussions, we realized something of the opportunity which such a group of Christians offer to Southern Baptists for effective cooperation in helping to carry the salvation of Christ to the Orient."

To him this emergence of strong churches, conventions, and leadership was a mark of the modern era with the greatest significance, calling for a re-examination of our missionary objective as Baptists and a recasting of the role of the missionary. Should our objective be so to control the development as to make Chinese and Japanese churches replicas of Southern Baptist churches and the conventions extensions of the Southern Baptist Convention? Or should our objective be to help the Oriental Baptists organize churches and conventions that would have the same independence and freedom to work out their life as we have? Shall we insist that they be in every way "Southern Baptists"? And should the missionary's role be the same as in pioneer situations in making programs, directing, and controlling? Or should he become a helper and counselor? So strongly did he feel the necessity of a definite answer to these questions that in his first secretarial report in the spring of 1937 he dwelt upon it.

He wrote,

I believe that it is in this development that Southern Baptists will be called on in the years immediately ahead of us to undertake the greatest adventure of faith we have been confronted with in our missionary work. With the increasing development of this Chinese consciousness Southern Baptists will need to know in a very real way the meaning of the words of Jesus, that "except a grain of wheat fall into the ground and die, it abideth alone, but if it die it beareth much fruit." As this Chinese Baptist consciousness grows, increasing Chinese initiative develops. As good Baptists these people insist in many instances on working out their own interpretations and positions through their growth and experience, even though in this process they be involved in painful errors. Certainly we have demanded this right in our own history. We shall see these Baptist people go at times in directions which will cause our hearts to sink within us. It is there that great faith is called for. How far shall we go with them in their wrong ways? Just where shall we refuse to go further with them? Truly we have a responsibility to help them to avoid some of the errors that we have made, and those which we are still making. The problems cannot be met by the use of a rule or a fixed policy. To meet them calls for a faith that enables one to fall into the ground and die.

Furthermore, this emerging Baptist consciousness makes it necessary that in our missionary work we be able to die unto ourselves as an American denomination. We cannot expect the institutions and churches which we promote in the Orient to be extensions of the Southern Baptist denomination in America. In the institutions of training we cannot expect to train Chinese to be good Southern Baptists, but we must expect them to be good Chinese Baptists who will be able under the direct guidance of the Holy Spirit to possess their own souls.

This did not mean that the missionaries would be any less Baptist or teach the doctrines of Baptists with any less conviction. It only meant that, having delivered his witness and his faith in his thought and practice, the missionary should grant to the other the freedom he claimed for himself without threat of withdrawal. The individual freedom and church autonomy of our Baptist polity should apply in an Oriental situation as in America.

Nor did it mean the reduction of the missionary enterprise. Everywhere in China and Japan the plea was for more missionaries. The one message to America was, "Send us more missionaries." There was never a greater need for missionary evangelists. To quote Dr. Rankin directly,

While we have done well to place upon the Chinese the responsibility for this work we have left them too much to do the work alone. We need missionaries who will give themselves again to the old method of country itinerating. There are unlimited opportunities for genuine help which such missionaries can give to the Chinese pastors and the evangelists who are located in chapels and churches throughout the country districts. The present unexcelled opportunities for direct evangelism demand that we give more emphasis to this type of work.

At the same time, he was bold to say that the most pressing need of the day was not to flood the Orient with foreign missionary evangelists. The major service of missionaries in the immediate future must be the re-enforcement of the native Christian constituencies. If the future of the Baptist denomination in the Orient lay with the Baptist churches of that area, then the greatest contribution Southern Baptists could make to that future would be in the development of strong churches and schools. Without a strong program of Christian education, without a leadership well grounded in biblical and theological understanding, the "impulse of experience" would result in impermanent and false interpretations of faith. Untaught Christians in the churches would remain as babes, and ignorant preachers in the pulpit would make even evangelism misrepresent the meaning of saving faith. Dr. Rankin said, "We need to remind ourselves anew that this is our task, even though it may materially reduce the total number of individuals whom we (personally) can win to Christ." Here was the challenge and here the point of most serious lag. Although most of the schools had survived the decade of upheaval and poverty, they were in poor condition and insufficiently staffed. He continued, "We do not have in any of our missions sufficient provisions for training

78

the Christian workers and leaders who are needed to carry on the work."

Just as the survey of the field was completed and plans for advance were getting under way there came the war between Japan and China. Suddenly in the summer of 1937 the Japanese armies began their invasion of China. Within weeks the whole picture was changed. By the hundreds of thousands the Chinese people were fleeing from death before the devastating horror, leaving behind all their material possessions. "I do not believe," wrote Dr. Rankin late in that year, "that ancient history has ever known a more cruel and savage scourge than that which has been spreading over China during these months. Families with small children and aged parents have been blasted from their homes and have been scattered all over the interior provinces seeking refuge and shelter. At times the paths and highways have been filled with thousands of these fleeing people who knew not where they went." Among them were many Christians whose homes and schools and churches were left in shambles or taken over for the invading armies.

In the alarm of these first months the missionaries had to face the question of evacuation. The United States government ordered home all women and children and others whose presence in China was not necessary. Loved ones in America were in a panic and the Foreign Mission Board shared their fear for the missionaries. Upon Dr. Rankin fell a major responsibility in making critical decisions and preserving morale as the whole work was thrown into confusion. His reaction to the situation is expressed in a letter to Dr. Maddry in September:

The Chinese Christians are suffering most in the disasters which are overtaking us, but we are finding that as missionaries our hearts and souls are being severely tried. One almost has to harden his capacity for sympathy and compassion to keep from being haunted by the tragedy and suffering to be seen on every hand. For those who love China and her people, a look into the future almost brings despair. The work of God's kingdom in our missions, the churches, schools, hospitals seem about to be swept away by the destroying hand of war. Our missionaries are being scattered here, there and everywhere, and in the end not a few of them will be lost to the work. I am especially apprehensive about our new missionaries in the North. I cannot get in close touch with them, and so do not know what they are thinking. They are being urged to withdraw from China. If they leave where will they go? Probably to America—and then what? . . . Still history teaches us and faith assures us that God's kingdom will go on, that his work, though crushed down, will rise up again with new life and vigor. Storms have come in the past, perhaps as severe as this one, and God's children have risen up after them to go forward into new undertakings in his service. I pray God to give us faith to endure with patience the trials of this storm so that we shall be able to rise up and go forward in his service when it has passed.

Neither he nor the other missionaries thought of giving up. At the Board's urging, some of them who were approaching retirement, those who were due a furlough, some who were not strong physically, and women with children withdrew. Dr. Rankin sympathized with those who consented to go home: "In doing so they are being just as loyal to the cause of Christ at this time as those of us who have the privilege of staying by the work on the field; in fact I think in many cases the personal sacrifice of those who go is perhaps greater than of those who stay." A member of the Foreign Board says that the only time he ever saw Dr. Rankin "blow his top" was when someone in a meeting called in question the courage and loyalty of those who returned home.

He spoke for the whole dedicated group when he said,

The outlook is dark but we are in no sense despairing. Whatever the conditions of the future we are going on with God's kingdom work. If we cannot follow one road we will find another. The saving gospel of Jesus Christ must be given to the people of the Orient, regardless of what the political situation may be. We may be disorganized for a time, and may have to make tremendous readjustments in our program and methods, but we will not stop. I do not believe there is the least feeling among the missionaries of giving up. "If God be for us who can be against us?"

The secretary would not be thrown into panic, or made to forget the soldierly terms on which a missionary enlists, or to consider his own fortune in the pursuit of duty. And his poise and courage, his understanding and unceasing solicitude for the safety of every missionary, his encouragement and hopefulness, his yearning to hold on had much to do with the sustained morale of those who worked with him.

A story he told about a little Chinese boy and himself illustrates the resilience of his faith and his pastoral heart in those trying times. While he was visiting one of the stations, a Japanese bombing squadron attacked the city. At a signal hundreds of people rushed for safety to a cavern beneath a hill. As they stood crowded together in semidarkness, the hill shook under a terrible bombardment. Suddenly he felt a little hand slip into his and heard a little boy asking anxiously, *"Pa um pa?"* (Afraid? Not afraid?). He was afraid! But in the moment between the question and his answer another world of reality came to mind, and with his own confidence renewed, he said firmly, *"Um pa"* (I'm not afraid!). And he was not, for he knew why he was there and under whose command.

81

In January, 1938, it had to be said that all normal missionary work in the occupied area was at a complete standstill. But as those areas were stablized under Japanese authority, work was resumed, even though under distressing conditions of poverty, restriction, and constant danger. Churches, depleted in membership and houseless, reassembled in homes or rented buildings; schools were opened in whatever space could be found; hospitals were reopened. The missionaries found opportunity for most fruitful service. The fact that they remained and shared their hardships undergirded the faith of Chinese Christians. Moreover, as always, the suffering of the people opened a door to their hearts and made them listen with yearning to the gospel.

In this period Dr. Rankin's constant prayer was that he might have the grace and insight to be realistic. One could easily become an unhappy pessimist in the face of the strong official Japanese opinion that missionaries are not needed and are not wanted, or one could be an optimist refusing to face facts. In the light of facts as he was able to see them, he suggested a fourfold procedure.

First, as far as possible the missionaries should remain in their stations, using whatever opportunities presented themselves, accepting "the authority of the Japanese while they controlled, and avoiding any involvement in political matters. Our one business is to present Christ as Savior and Lord to people sorely in need. . . . We must not give up in the occupied zones because of limitations."

He applauded heartily the missionary who, forced to leave his station, at the first opportunity announced that he was returning. Friends reminded him of the dangers and restrictions: the city was under martial law, he could not hold church services or preach on the street, he could not have classes or groups in his own house. "I know all that," he replied. "Well, then," they asked, "what do you intend to do when you go back?" His answer was, "Why, man alive, I am just going to *be* there!"

Second, we immediately should push on into new fields in the provinces that lay toward the west. The government of China had been moved to Chungking (Szechuan Province); hundreds of thousands of people had moved to the southwest; and in all probability the Japanese would not overrun these areas. Large numbers of Christian leaders and professional and businessmen would begin over again there. Moreover, in large sections there was little or no Christian work of any kind. Baptists, therefore, had a great opportunity and responsibility to plant the Christian faith in this "Free China." The idea was that some of the strongest missionaries should go at once to select strategic new fields for missionary service.

Third, in the missionary program fresh consideration should be given to the importance of the local church. Not only historic Baptist doctrine but many facts of experience in recent years called for this reconsideration. One was the increasing limitations upon other forms of Christian institutions; another was the growing dependence upon the churches for spread of the gospel; and another, the trend in highly organized Christian groups to ignore the significance of the local church in Christian advance. After wide conference and at the request of a number of fellow workers, Dr. Rankin wrote a letter in November, 1938, to all the missions, embodying his idea, particularly in its relation to the missionary educational program:

There is a growing conviction that the conditions which are now being produced in China call for a renewed emphasis upon the essential place of local churches in the Kingdom program. In the general discussions and thinking concerning missionary work in China during the past years, we have come to think largely of the "Christian Movement." To many people this "Christian Movement" is made up of various kinds of Christian undertakings—educational work, medical work, evangelistic work, etc. Questions have been asked as to whether the churches, after all, are an essential part of the "Christian Movement."

Some of us believe that an outstanding imperative in Kingdom work today is to return to a recognition of the foundational place which local churches occupy in the Kingdom movement. We believe that all other forms of mission work should be weighed and measured in terms of their relationship to the churches. Local churches are the source and fountainhead of the Kingdom work. We believe that they are the agencies which Christ ordained for the extension of the Kingdom on earth. These churches are the stove which will keep boiling the various pots which we call Christian education, medical work, etc. When the heat of these churches (the stove) cools off the various pots in time cease to be "hot" as Christian institutions.

In our Southern Baptist mission work in China, I believe that we are being presented with an opportunity to reconsider carefully our educational work with reference to its relation to the local churches. Some of our mission schools are confronting serious problems at the present time in the large number of students who want to enter them. If we are not careful, we can easily be led into undertaking to educate the children of China. This we cannot possibly do, and I do not believe that this is in any sense the task of Christian missions. Many of us are convinced that our educational task is to teach and train Christian people for service and train church members to live and function as Christians. . . . This opinion was growing in strength before the outbreak of the present hostilities. It seems now that the situation which is developing in this country will make such a plan imperative. Circumstances may force us to devote a considerable part of our whole mission program to the work of elementary teaching and training of church members for active Christian service in and through churches. Indications now are that we shall find larger opportunities and fewer difficulties in this type of work than in any other form of mission work. More and more we have come to believe that this is the greatest need in the life of the churches and in Kingdom work in China today.

Fourth, along with the emphasis on elementary education for Christian living must go an enlargement of advanced pastoral and leadership education. In 1935 Dr. Maddry had given his support to the proposed establishment of a central all-China Baptist theological seminary for middle school and college graduates, but it had been necessarily postponed. That and other plans for theological training should now be revived.

In the spring of 1939 Dr. Rankin called a meeting in Kaifeng (interior China) of representatives of all the missions and of the affiliated Chinese Baptist conventions for the consideration of the whole Baptist undertaking. It was a most significant meeting. Definite plans were made for the opening of an advanced theological school in Kaifeng, for increased production and distribution of Christian literature through the China Baptist Publication Society, and for a China-wide evangelistic campaign in 1940.

The spirit and conviction that stirred this meeting are expressed in a letter from Dr. Rankin to all the missionaries:

God had an experience for us which no one anticipated. Indeed, some of us went to Kaifeng with considerable discouragement and misgiving about the wisdom of projecting any kind of forward movement in China at this time. Our vision and outlook had been largely colored by the experiences of the war. But we had not long been in the conference before we found ourselves wrestling with the Lord. Every one present became conscious of a lead not of ourselves, that seemed to point in a direction which our own judgment hesitated to follow. . . . We were confronted with a deep conviction that in this time of uncertainty God would not have us stand still. . . . We could not hold back because of the possibility of failure. . . . In this conviction we determined to go as far as we can. If our plans are frustrated we shall not have failed in our faith. . . . We cannot permit the vision of a united witness of Baptists throughout China to fade. Plans and programs may have to be changed, but these responses will abide and will give new impetus to our work.

With this the first phase of Dr. Rankin's leadership in the Orient was completed. He and the entire missionary force had become one in spirit and vision. Three years of war conditions had been weathered, the task had been defined more definitely, horizons had been lifted, and a program of advance had created new enthusiasms. Of necessity China claimed first attention in this period. But in Japan there was steady progress in the mission and in the churches. The Baptists of the two warring countries displayed a mutuality of understanding and sympathy, and the roots of faith and purpose were deepened for the ordeal through which the Japanese Baptists and the missionaries there would soon be called upon to endure.

VI

SECRETARY FOR THE ORIENT

(*Continued*) 1940–44

Soon after the uplift of the Kaifeng conference and its momentous decisions, the time came for Dr. Rankin to return to America for a year, as agreed upon when he was elected secretary (three years on the field, one at home). He was reluctant to leave, but the Board felt that he was needed greatly at home to give to the people a clearer view of the missionary situation in the Orient and to get for himself needed relaxation from his wearing responsibilities on the field. But from the time the family was settled in Richmond in July, his heart longed to return to the Orient. Dr. Maddry and the Board tried to gain his consent to transfer his headquarters to Richmond, to spend three years there and one in the Orient. He managed to postpone any final decision on the matter, and before his year was out he returned to China.

The months in America were profitable for him and for the cause of missions. There was a growing skepticism about Oriental missions in view of war conditions—the uncertainty about China and a great resentment against the Japanese. Dr. Rankin did much through public address and the press to combat this crippling and, as he thought from the Christian standpoint, unwarranted attitude. For one thing, he cited the ways in which the mission work was going forward, the spirit of the missionaries, the heroism and faithfulness of the Christian people, and the increased response to the gospel witness everywhere, showing that the enterprise was far from futile. He wrote articles and spoke about the motivation of missions, the dynamic of missions, the indestructibility of missions. He gave the point of view of the missionaries who, like Paul, were held to their posts because they were in the grip of the love of Christ, who gave his life for men, suffering death for his enemies. His challenge everywhere was for faith in the love, power, and purpose of Jesus Christ:

This dynamic of love, this power of the gospel of Jesus Christ, which is able to save the people of the Orient and of the whole world, dwells not in buildings and institutions which can be destroyed by wars but in the hearts of men and women. God's kingdom cannot wait on the outcome of wars and the decisions of nations. When the power of the love of Christ constrains us, has hold of us, we cannot wait or mark time until the war is over to hear the call of the present opportunities in the Orient. We must go *now;* we must send missionaries *now;* we must give of our means and ourselves *now.*

Leaving his family in America, he returned to the Orient in May, 1940. In October he received a cablegram from Dr. Maddry stating that the Board was unanimously of the opinion that he should return as soon as possible and transfer his headquarters to Richmond. Again he was faced on one hand with the alternative of comparative safety, the easier road, union with his family; and, on the other, with the hazards and problems of remaining where he was. His choice was the latter. His reply was more diplomatic than a refusal, but it indicated his mind:

I do not think we have ever confronted a time when it was more imperative that someone with the authority of the Board be here on the spot. If I were still in America, I am certain that it would be necessary for the Board to get me out here. I feel certain that you and the Board have taken all this into consideration in proposing that the Board's action take effect "as soon as possible." It goes without saying so that I cannot possibly leave here until this present crisis has been handled. I believe you and the Board will agree with me that my first duty and responsibility is to see our work in the Orient through this crisis. At the moment I am unable to see any farther than that.

In addition to resuming his share of responsibility in implementing the resolutions passed in Kaifeng in 1939, trying to settle problems—property, restrictions, and other —with the Japanese authorities, and efforts at rehabilitation of churches and schools in the occupied areas of China, he was greatly concerned about the missionary situation in Japan.

During the first years of the war with China our mission in Japan was able to pursue its normal activities, since the United States was not involved. But in 1940 the Japanese announced the Christian movement would be integrated with the New National Structure. Nobody knew just what that would mean. There was a general understanding that it would call for a united Christian Church, that all Christian activities would be controlled and supported by Japanese without foreign aid, and that all Christian schools must, as parts of the new structure, foster the Japanese spirit. It seemed that soon there would be little place for missionaries or for separate denominations. Japanese nationalism was becoming totalitarian in its demands.

About the same time, questions were raised about the girls' school in Kokura where two missionaries taught. The school was on a high point of ground that commanded a good view of one of Japan's most important fortified zones. The rising tension between Japan and America was reflected in the demand by some in the area that the school be removed or the American missionaries be dismissed. The two missionary teachers and all missionary members of the board of trustees withdrew, and the particular trouble subsided. The incident, however, only emphasized the questions raised by the new structure about the future. Should we close the mission and withdraw the missionaries? If the Japanese Baptists should be forced to become a part of a National Christian Church, should we desert them? At home some were answering with a quick yes as soon as they heard.

In early September Dr. Rankin went to Japan to appraise the situation. He was convinced after many conferences that the Japanese Baptists would have to co-operate with a national church but would not have to relinquish their denominational identity or program; that missionaries would be limited in their service but would not be forced out; and also that the Baptist leaders were very anxious to have the counsel of the trusted missionaries and the sympathetic understanding and confidence of Southern Baptists. One leader said, "We have come now to a place where we Japanese Christians may have to walk alone. We do not know just where we are going. We must try to understand the situation and then make the best decisions we can. As we go we want your patience and your sympathy." The president of the Japanese convention said, "Tell them [Southern Baptists] that the time has come now when we may not be able to accept longer all the aid they have been giving to us. It is our hope, however, that this discontinuance of financial relationship will in no way affect our spiritual relationship. We need their patience. We hope they will not make hasty decisions. We must find our way and we shall need patience as we make mistakes in finding that way. Assure them, please, that in whatever changes we may make, we shall try to be loyal to our faith in God." Neither Dr. Rankin nor the missionaries felt that any immediate decisions should be made.

After several months he went again to Japan for further conferences with the missionaries. In the light of developments, it was decided that the recently appointed missionaries be relocated in China or elsewhere, but that the older workers—the Doziers and Garretts and Miss Lancaster—remain to maintain the mission and continue a distinctively Baptist witness. They would stand ready to be of every possible assistance to the Japanese Baptists as they worked out their problem. This was an hour of testing for all concerned.

In explaining this decision, which was a recommendation to the Foreign Mission Board, Dr. Rankin wrote:

In this day when the ideals of totalitarianism are having such widespread influence on Christian thinking and when so many outstanding leaders of Christian thought are thinking in terms of "ecclesiastical solidarity," I believe we are confronted with the duty of giving an isolated emphasis to the necessity of individual experience and responsibility to God. More and more it seems that such a task and duty is being left largely to Southern Baptists. I would not imply that we think the belief in individual experience and responsibility is entirely lacking on the part of Christian people who work for organic church unity, but I do believe that the emphasis upon this conviction is largely lost under the weight of "ecclesiastical solidarity." By confining our resources in personnel and finances to work that is distinctively Baptist, we shall be in a position to place our emphasis positively at that point.

91

He had expressed the same conviction after the Madras Conference (which he and Dr. Maddry attended) a year earlier: "I have returned from the Madras Conference all the more firm in my conviction that as Baptists we are going to give our message to the world most effectively by remaining Baptist."

At the same time, the recommendation registered a desire to co-operate as far as possible with the Japanese Baptists and the whole Christian movement in Japan, so long as this could be done without muffling our distinctive points of view. This spirit had been manifested by him in China in relation to the National Christian Council, in his participation in the Madras Conference, and appeared later in relation to the Foreign Missions Conference. His altogether brotherly spirit was reflected in a letter to Dr. B. J. Cauthen and others who were active in establishing a new mission in Free China: "We should confer with other mission organizations operating in West China so that we will not create difficulties for ourselves and for those other organizations with reference to mission cooperation."

From the summer of 1941 another cloud over our work in the Orient was growing rapidly. Tension between Japan and the United States was almost at the breaking point. The Asiatic War (since 1937) and the European War (since 1939) might at any time be merged into a world war which would engulf all missions. Meanwhile, the program already mapped out was being pushed. On November 2, Dr. Rankin wrote from Hong Kong as he was about to fly to Shiuchow and thence to Kweilin in Free China:

It appears to me that the next few weeks will be the most critical days we have thus far faced in the Far East. I cannot help but question whether I shall be able to get back to Shanghai, or even Hong Kong. By the middle of December all our people in the occupied areas may have been caught in the outbreak of war. In the light of these possibilities I am asking very seriously if we have been right in going on with the work as we have done, and I want to say again that I do not see how we could have done anything else.

He did get back to Hong Kong, but not to Shanghai. On December 7 came the Japanese attack on Pearl Harbor, and our whole missionary enterprise entered a new and darker day.

Dr. Rankin was in Hong Kong at the time, having flown in from Kweilin, hoping to get back to Shanghai. This he was unable to do, and after "Pearl Harbor" he was interned. A hero story got started to the effect that he delayed his departure from Kweilin in order to take with him missionary Oz Quick, who had been ill with appendicitis. This he denied with some impatience, "Nothing to it. I took the first available plane. Oz was in a Hong Kong hospital when I arrived." Hong Kong was taken by the Japanese on Christmas Day, and all Baptists and Americans became prisoners. Besides Dr. Rankin, five Southern Baptist missionaries were among them: the Cecil Wards, Miss Flora Dodson, Miss Orris Pender, and Oz Quick.

For two or three weeks before the fall of Hong Kong this group was billeted in an apartment house well up the peak from the harbor and were not too uncomfortable, except for the hazards of the Japanese bombardment. They were supposed to remain indoors, but one day, food having given out, Dr. Rankin ventured out to make some purchases. As he walked down a street, a group of Japanese soldiers suddenly appeared. What should he do? His first impulse was to run. But on second thought he decided that conversation would be better than bullets. So, concealing his fear, he walked on toward them. Of course, they stopped him and grilled him with questions. When they asked him what his business was in China, he explained that he was a Christian missionary. One of the men asked with evident interest, "Are you Christian?" When he replied yes, the man reached out his hand and said, "I Christian, too." With that, he was permitted to go on his way. There is no need for comment on the significance of an experience like that.

The day came when all the prisoners, British and American, were lined up and marched to Stanley Prison, where concentration camp life began in earnest. Our missionaries were not put in the old prison but in buildings formerly occupied by the wardens. But the other could not have been much worse. Nothing made for comfort. There were six men or women in each room. They had no furniture or furnishings of any kind. Only after several months did they have cots to sleep on. It was left to the prisoners to organize their own life, take care of the premises, cook, wash, provide clothing, etc. The Japanese or turncoat Chinese only stood guard.

The American group, about three hundred in all, formed a commune, with a council of twelve members in "command" to preserve an orderly existence. Dr. Rankin was chosen as a member of the council and assigned to the food department. He spent much time at it, often himself baking the bread for the entire group. Food soon became a real problem; the supplies were meager and of the poorest sort. Under ordinary conditions the meat and rice would not have been used. Even the most circumspect persons came to the point where to steal was a great temptation. One day Dr. Rankin caught a missionary stealing food for himself and, for more reasons than one, felt like "beating the tar out of him." One reporter said of the condition, "The internes of Stanley Prison were being starved to death by slow stages." In the months at Stanley Dr. Rankin lost thirty pounds that he could hardly spare.

The missionaries had Chinese Christian friends who obtained permission to bring them baskets of supplies once a month. One day Dr. Rankin received a small jar of jelly; and a missionary family, some flour. They pooled their riches for a feast of biscuits and jelly, but when Dr. Rankin saw how eagerly the children of the family enjoyed the jelly, he ate only biscuits. The faithful friendship of the Christians outside and the fellowship with Christians inside the prison helped to make life brighter. There was an occasional book, and always the Book. There was the renewal of spirit through worship; there was space for exercise and sunshine; there were diversions of various sorts, some useful. One man was very clever with his hands and could convert rubbish of all sorts into useful articles. Dr. Rankin's shoes were badly worn, and the man offered to show him how to make a pair by hollowing out the shape of his foot in pieces of wood and using strips of an old rubber tire to hold them on. Not too long afterward he was clop-clopping around in wooden shoes.

Thus life went on amid want and both physical and mental sickness. Gaunt forms became more gaunt. They were shut out from the world except for a smuggled letter now and then and newspapers that printed more error than truth. It was a wondrously happy day, therefore, when news came that arrangements were completed for the Americans to go home in exchange for Japanese prisoners. They had given up hope of being released before the war ended.

In July, 1942, Dr. Rankin and thirty-nine other Southern Baptist missionaries started home, greatly worn but with stout hearts. On board ship he wrote to Dr. Maddry,

It is useless to say that all of us are happy beyond expression in the prospect of reaching our homes. Some of us feel that we have been delivered from most distressing circumstances and our joy in deliverance is great. At the same time I do not believe a single one of us could wish that our decisions in remaining in the Orient had been different. We are coming home with the conviction that we tried to be true to the leadership of our Lord, and that our coming home now is in no sense a defeat. Among our group I find no lack of confidence or faith in the leadership of our Lord. We are conscious that in all the chaos about us God is working out his will; and we gladly follow his lead when we are unable to see the way ahead.

The *Gripsholm,* to which the missionaries were transferred en route, reached New York in August. Although the physicians and the Board prescribed a leisurely and long period of rest and recreation, Dr. Rankin could not long be kept inactive. The long ocean voyage and the restorative power of being united with his family had done much to revive his energies. And the people wanted to hear him. After a few weeks, therefore, without waiting to regain his lost thirty pounds, he was accepting engagements to speak and busying himself with his secretarial duties. He could not forget what a soldier had said to him in New York. This soldier noticed the word "Gripsholm" on a piece of luggage, and when Dr. Rankin informed him that he had just arrived from the East, he replied, "I'll soon be pushing out where you have come from; we've got a job to do out there." The "job out there" could not be laid aside.

There was also an inner urge to bear witness to the fresh

realization of spiritual resources that he had experienced. This he recalled:

Our group of missionaries [in Hong Kong] had been placed in an apartment house on a peak on which a great part of the city of Hong Kong is built. Just above the apartment house, in the ground, were many gun emplacements. The Japanese kept it under constant fire. It was difficult for us to understand how the building missed direct hits, for literally hundreds of shells and bombs fell about it. One day we were standing outside. With us was a Chinese cook who had lived in that apartment and had stayed with us throughout the siege. Many times we had talked with him about Christ, but he was not a Christian. As we stood there that day looking at the destruction all about us, the cook said, "Look! There's a ring around this building!" Then he added, "God put this ring around this building because you are here and because you are his servants." Here is the testimony: At the moment I was constrained to say, "I'm not so sure of that." I did not want to leave that cook with the impression that if we project our lives in loyalty to Jesus Christ he promises that we will not suffer from the dangers about us. Yes, we could have been killed, and God still would have been faithful. I am persuaded that there are times when he sees fit to do precisely that thing. However, since coming back to America, everywhere I go I hear the refrain, "We prayed for you. We prayed for you." A few days after I got back to Richmond a friend asked, "Have you realized yet what it means to have been prayed for by name by literally hundreds of thousands of people?" Well, I am in the midst of realizing it, and I am persuaded that God did put that ring about that building.

In all that he did afterwards two things always stood out in bold emphasis: our resources in God and the power of prayer. These he had believed; now in his heart he knew them as the very foundations of spiritual and missionary advance.

He returned, therefore, stronger in soul, if not in body, and with fresh dedication and hope. He was not permitted to return to the Orient, but rendered invaluable service in Richmond and throughout the Convention, in the interest of the "job out there." At the October meeting of the Foreign Mission Board he was actively at work with a committee to make new plans for work in the Orient. In the same month articles from his pen began to appear in the Baptist papers. One of them rather surprisingly, but characteristically, bore the title "Good News from the Orient." It was good news of strong hope that our other missionaries in Japanese hands soon would be returned home; good news of progress being made by our missionaries in Free China; but most of all, good news about the Chinese and Japanese Christians who, without the aid of missionaries, were carrying on in occupied China and, where necessary, were transferring their schools to Free China and rebuilding their own Christian program there. He was saying that we have reason to be strong of heart and to keep our eyes to the front.

That, rather than discouragement or defeatism, was the mood of his service in the homeland in 1943 and 1944. None appreciated the meaning of his presence and his outlook and passion more than Dr. Maddry, under whose leadership he worked. His interpretation of the world situation, his own tested experience, his deep conviction concerning the denomination's duty, his conception of the meaning of missions and of the urgency of the present challenge of Christ proved a tonic for our people and had much to do with their increasing response to the world task.

One of Dr. Rankin's cares in the homeland was the missionaries with whom he had shared many hardships and who now, like himself, were displaced persons in America and the Philippines or still in captivity, wanting to return to their work. One of the things that had won him respect and greatly endeared him to his co-workers was his pastoral concern. In his first definition of his office he had included "sharing with individual missionaries their problems and needs" and promoting among them a spiritual unity that was necessary to effective co-operation. Like a good pastor, he often undergirded those who became discouraged, and like a good pastor he sometimes called to repentance.

Also like a good pastor, he sometimes could become adamant in his insistence upon the spiritual qualities necessary in Christian service. On one occasion he had written to Dr. Maddry about a particularly unhappy situation in which strong personal attitudes and hot tempers had created a distressing disharmony; and he had risked his own popularity by insisting upon the necessity of reconciliation. He wrote: "I cannot shut my eyes to such conditions and feel that I am honest with reference to the work out here or to the Foreign Mission Board. . . . I may find that I shall create some serious problems trying to put such a conviction into effect, but I am not willing to accept that this cannot be done." This was an extreme and rare situation, but it reveals his unselfish commitment to the ministry of reconciliation and to the conviction that in the service of Christ we ourselves should possess the spirit of the Christ we serve. It was this combination of friendliness and frankness, of willingness to face every sort of personal problem with sympathy, love, and truth that made him (to quote a missionary's tribute) "every missionary's pastor."

The same personal and spiritual concern was a part of his ministry while in America. Some of those who had returned home found pastorates, some did deputation work, some became teachers or engaged in evangelistic meetings. Many wanting to return to the field were restless and confused. By personal contacts and letters Dr. Rankin did much to strengthen courage and patience. A letter to one of our finest missionaries is typical of that ministry. In part it said:

It is not our responsibility, however, to explain all of these circumstances. During the past few years I have learned that as servants of God we come again and again face to face with situations which are beyond our power to determine and in which God requires only that we accept the situation as a fact and make the best adjustment we can to it. Over and over we have seen a door close, a road impassably blocked, a hopeful plan made utterly impossible. In such situations we have been compelled to accept the facts as they are without explanations and without answers to our many questions.

I realize that you do not need to be told of such circumstances. Truly you have had to face a number of them for yourself during the past few years. It is just that kind of thing that you are facing now. But you will not have to face it alone. In the first place, God will help you in this instance as He has in the past to make your readjustments. Dr. Maddry and I will face it with you, also.

I shall add a word of admonition. For the present, let the whole matter rest. Do not give yourself concern at all about the fact that you are not able to go back to China at this time. You cannot help the situaion by worrying about that which you cannot possibly determine. I learned a little from the internment camp in this respect. I found myself confined in a situation that was not at all to my liking. I very much wanted to get out of it, but it did not take me long to accept without any question that it would be useless for me to lunge at those barbed wire barriers and against the bayonets surrounding them in an attempt to break out. There was nothing for me to do but to accept the situation, relax, and make the best of the place I was in until such time as I could get out. Now that is my little sermon for whatever it may be worth.

It fell to Dr. Rankin also to help present to the denomination the call of the Board for three things in its plans for the present and postwar program in the Orient: relief and rehabilitation, enlisting recruits, and building up a financial reserve beyond current support for the day of new opportunity. It was his spirit in this service that recalled what some had already called him—the secretary *from* the Orient. His heart was in China and Japan and his presentation of their needs burned deep with passion.

As he spoke in churches, schools, and conventions, men were not impressed by any masterly presence or oratorical manner. He seemed rather shy and tense. He was no rabble-rouser; he did not stir now laughter, now tears. But there was an eloquence that captured heart and mind with a clear burning light. William Wirt said of Chief Justice John Marshall, "This extraordinary man without the aid of fancy, the advantages of person, voice, attitudes, gesture or any of the ornaments of an orator, deserves to be considered as one of the most eloquent men of the world, if eloquence may be said to consist of the power of seizing the attention with irresistible force and never permitting it to elude its grasp until the hearer has received the conviction which the speaker intends." In that definition of eloquence Dr. Rankin was an eloquent advocate of world missions.

The relation of Southern Baptists to Christ's world mission was his one theme. His mastery of facts about us at home and abroad, his exposition of Christ's purpose, the intensity and boldness of his convictions, the forthrightness of his challenge gave to him great persuasive power. He rallied the small rural churches by making them see that any church is great that binds itself heartily to the world mission of Christ and challenged the city churches by his equally strong conviction that no church is great that does not bind itself with all its might to that mission. His much-used text was, "For whosoever will save his life shall lose it; but whosoever shall lose his life for my sake and the gospel's, the same shall save it."

His addresses were a personal challenge. They were not overburdened with exhortation, but his own vivid sense of the claim of facts and truth upon his own life was communicated to those who heard him. He did not storm the emotions so much as bring them under the warming and often burning light of the world's need, God's intention, and our involvement in it all. It was this illuminating and penetrating personal quality that challenged the minds and hearts of men and women to accept their share in a world mission that was their own.

The personnel department of the Board found great help in his work with college and seminary students. In that difficult time when the doors of China and Japan were shut and the whole world was at war, one of the objectives of the Board was to build a reserve of recruits who would be ready at the war's end. In this difficult task Dr. Rankin, with his long experience in the Orient, climaxed by his imprisonment, was able to speak with peculiar power. The unheroic hero, who transcended all questions of personal fortune in his presentation of the claims of Christ and the kingdom of God, challenged them with our Lord's unqualified demand, "If any man will come after me, let him deny himself, and take up his cross, and follow me." This he called upon them to do, not blindfolded, but in the light of all the hard facts of the present world situation; and about these he was very frank. He held before them the rough roads along which mission history had come. He interpreted to them the objectives of missionary service as he had come to see them. He reminded them that all things that could be changed were changing and that there was the necessity for a new missionary to have wisdom and courage to hold on to some old things and lay hold of new things, new ideas and methods, untried in the past. The way which he pointed out was built on real experience.

In a series of five lectures to the students of the New Orleans Seminary in 1943 he elaborated these ideas, climaxing the whole with a lecture on "Resources for the Task in the New Day." And the resources he talked about to the students were not the resources we have in God. To be sure, in God we have all our resources; "out of him, and through him, and unto him are all things." But in the present crisis of spiritual warfare—God's war against sin—he chose to speak to students and all Southern Baptists of the resources in us that God is calling for.

Over and over again he referred to our part in World War II and our acquiescence in the demands of our government for men by the millions for military service, the marshaling of industry, billions of dollars in taxes, the gearing of every resource of the nation to win the war—all of that because we believed the preservation of the American way of life was worth it. Then he asked,

Is it madness, is it foolishness to think of Christians doing that kind of thing for the kingdom of God? . . . Let me ask this. Suppose one hundred of our missionaries had been caught in the Orient and killed. People would be saying, "It was foolish! They should not have done it." We send millions of men across the seas knowing that tens of thousands of them are not coming back. We do that to preserve the American way of life. How important is it to preserve God's way of life?

103

In every way in which he was called to serve in the plans of the Board he gave the strength of his experience and testimony. He was one of a far-visioned team. Dr. Maddry as leader was farsighted and dynamic in his leadership. Dr. George Sadler and Dr. Everett Gill, Jr., the other regional secretaries, were making equally vivid and compelling the needs of the other areas of our world task. The members of the staff, the missionaries at home from the field, mission-minded pastors, laymen, and women of faith and vision—all united to make 1943 and 1944 years of undergirding the denomination for missionary expansion.

In October, 1943, Dr. Maddry announced to the Board that he wished to retire from the executive secretaryship at the end of 1944, upon completion of twelve years of service. He felt that the task ahead in reorganization, administration, and expansion would "require the boundless strength and energy of a younger man." Very reluctantly the Board acceded to his wishes and appointed a committee to nominate his successor. At its first meeting the committee decided to look outside the Board's staff of secretaries for the new leader, wishing not to disturb the present excellent organization or hazard in any way the camaraderie that prevailed. The next meeting of the committee was in May, 1944, in Atlanta, while the Southern Baptist Convention was in session. It was proposed that before any nomination or discussion there should first be a season of prayer and that there should be a ballot on which each man would name his first choice. When the ballots were read, the name of M. Theron Rankin was found on every one. At its meeting in June the Board elected Dr. Rankin unanimously.

In explanation of his acceptance, he wrote to his co-worker, Frank Connelly,

I disagreed decidedly with the proposal to fill the position of Executive Secretary by taking the Secretary for the Orient for this place. I argued strongly that the needs for my services as Secretary for the Orient were greater than the needs for my services as Executive Secretary. When a man becomes convinced, however, that God is definitely leading him toward a certain end, it is no longer the prerogative of that man to argue and to reason as to which is the more needy or important place; his obligation and duty is to follow the lead of his Lord. In the end I reached this very definite conviction, and there was nothing for me to do but follow.

In January, 1945, he assumed his responsibilities as executive secretary, to become in the providence of God the leader in a new and greater chapter of denominational vision and adventure.

LEADERSHIP IN THE HOMELAND
1945–53

There were many things in the missionary picture in 1945 to give courage and hope to a new leader. The fact that the Southern Baptist Convention and the Foreign Mission Board were entering their second century of service was an incentive to gird for a greater future. Under the superb leadership of Dr. Maddry the Board had recovered fully from the long depression, and its work at home and abroad was so well organized as to require no essential change. The members of the Board, deeply committed to the cause of missions, gave assurance of seasoned counsel and guidance. Sharing in the secretarial responsibilities, Dr. Sadler, Dr. Gill, and Dr. Cauthen brought to their regional tasks all that could be desired in ability, outlook, and dedication. These, together with an able administrative and promotional staff in the home office, constituted a strong team, closely united in spirit and purpose.

By that time also the denomination was advancing in numbers and resources. Churches were multiplying, and the programs of the churches, state conventions, and of the Southern Baptist Convention were being expanded. The increase of the Lottie Moon Offering and private designations to foreign missions gave evidence that the sense of world mission was taking on new life. Every circumstance gave hope that if world missions could be taken from the margin and made central in their thinking, Southern Baptists would enter upon an epoch-making advance in their missionary enterprise.

Although in larger areas the situation remained critical, on the mission fields there was promise of better things. World War II was nearing its end, reviving hope that China and Japan soon would be open again. There were 504 missionaries under appointment to nineteen national areas. In seven countries in Latin America the work of more than two hundred missionaries was advancing steadily. The growth in Brazil was an inspiration. The African mission, with seventy-one missionaries, was asking for a hundred. In the exigencies of war a large group of missionaries, waiting to return to their fields, had opened work in Hawaii that would become permanent. And other areas were in the picture for future occupation.

Dr. Rankin was a well-chosen man for leadership in such a time. His twenty-four years of experience had given him an intimate acquaintance with missionary life and the problems and methods of administration. In spirit he was as thoroughly missionary as a man could be. Although he was born an American he was a citizen of the world. When asked what sort of man he had been, Mrs. Rankin replied, "He was just an ordinary man with the world in his heart." So thoroughly missionary was his outlook that he brought everything—doctrine, attitude, purpose, practice—under the test of its relation to, and its fitness for, the Christian world mission. In his thought, life and mission were inseparable in the Christian calling, and every Christian group, whether local church, association, state convention, or denominational group, should be conscious of being bound vitally to that world mission. And he believed thoroughly that once South-

107

ern Baptists became fully aroused to their calling they would, with their resources and their interpretation of the gospel, be able to serve the kingdom of God in a measure beyond any present dream.

At his first meeting with the administrative staff Dr. Rankin made clear what might be expected of him in his new office. He spoke of the comradeship they had enjoyed in the past as members of the same team, and said, "Every team has to have a captain. That is all I am. We will work together for the world program of Southern Baptists." He accepted the responsibilities of leadership, but he did so in such a way as to emphasize the comradeship rather than his new position. He thought of his office as functional and in no sense hierarchical. Some of his well-meaning friends suggested that as executive secretary he should dress a little differently and deport himself in carriage and dignity more like a man of position! But he was more amused than impressed. He would never be anything but a missionary, a member of the team, an individual in community doing his share in the common task. On their part, the staff and the missionaries accepted his leadership without losing any of the sense of nearness and personalness in their relations.

In this chapter three aspects of his secretaryship will be presented: as administrator, as interpreter, and as the advocate of advance.

His former experience in the field as teacher, treasurer, and regional secretary fitted him well for administrative duties. It taught him, for one thing, to regard every missionary dollar as something sacred and to be sacredly handled. From the time it was placed in the collection plate until, through pastor, teacher, evangelist, physician, nurse, Bible, or pamphlet, it brought peace and hope to a lost and broken spirit, it was a sacred trust. He knew its value and its meaning. For that reason he was in hearty agreement with the established tradition of the Board that its affairs should be conducted according to the requirements of sound business procedure.

For one thing, he believed that in all its plans and operations the Board should adhere to the principle of truth, or realism. Sober calculation, not wishful anticipation, must be the basis of action. That was good business. In a meeting of a planning committee one day someone asked him how many missionaries were needed in a certain field. When surprise was expressed at his conservative estimate, he answered, "I was speaking in terms of what we might be able to accomplish." He knew well the aching hearts of missionaries and the poignant needs in all the fields, but he knew also that not these, nor his own present desire, but the actual response of Southern Baptists was the measure of appropriation. Nor did his twenty-four years in the Orient obscure the fact that every part of the program must be planned in the light of the whole.

It was good faith and good business also for the Board to build up a reserve fund to safeguard the enterprise against such disasters as it had suffered in the 1930's, and he defended it against those who criticized it. To him it was more presumption than faith to leave the missionaries and institutions unprotected against the unpredictable hazards of economic change. A reserve fund reflected a responsible faith and in the course of years would mean more substantial progress. He rejected the method of the "faith missions" as paying too little attention to strong foundations of support at home and to laying strong foundations for an enduring church life and witness abroad. To the enthusiasms of faith must be added the wisdom of faith if stewards are to "walk in truth."

If reality was his first principle of administration, the second was responsibility—individual responsibility in particular assignments and joint responsibility in the common concern and total program of the Board. In his esteem the personnel of the Board, from the janitor to the latest appointed missionary, was a brotherhood of responsible persons. This meant that he trusted everyone to "bear his own burden"—a fact that saved him tensions and sleepless nights. On his part he assumed the full responsibility for performing the duties of executive secretary as defined by the Board.

Some things could not be delegated to others. For example, a very knotty problem in educational policy had arisen in Nigeria, and the Foreign Mission Board appointed three of its members to go and study the needs of the field and the particular problem. Someone representing a group wrote in strong disagreement, "We feel that the commission is not necessary, and, if it is, that persons other than those on the Board should go." To this Dr. Rankin replied simply, "The Southern Baptist Convention has committed responsibilities to the Foreign Mission Board which the Board must assume." The same was held to be true of everyone connected with the Board. "It is required in stewards, that a man be found faithful."

Equally important was the assumption of joint responsibility that called for counsel and free participation in reaching agreement on matters of common concern. Perhaps it was at this point more than at any other that Dr. Rankin's administrative procedure received most comment. At executive committee meetings and meetings of the staff and committees he sought from every member the free expression

110

of opinion and depended on the wisdom of the group. Dr. Truett once remarked about a prominent missionary leader, "He is eminently willing to have his own way." Not so Dr. Rankin. He excelled in his co-operative spirit. It was said by those who sat with him that he was willing to lay his own ideas on the table with the ideas of others and have them considered together on their merits, and he accepted the conclusions reached through free discussion. He did not require that his proposals come up as he had laid them down. That did not mean that he was weak in the defense of his own ideas. He argued for them as he expected others to argue for theirs. But the discussions were kept at the level that aimed at common agreement rather than defeat or victory for any man. Along this road of mutuality and freedom, the organization at home and abroad enjoyed a remarkable unity of spirit.

Another characteristic of the period of Dr. Rankin's administration was enterprise—enterprise on the field in response to the urgency of the time. With the ending of World War II, the entire force of workers was alert to the opportunities of the new day. Within a week after the surrender of Japan, representative missionaries met in Richmond to plan for the reprojection of missionary work in the devastated areas. Within thirty days after V-J Day, missionaries were back in Shanghai, to be followed by an increasing stream. Contact was established with the Baptists of Japan through the offices of a United States chaplain, and missionaries were ready to fly from Hawaii as soon as the occupation authority would permit.

The first two years after the war were marked by extensive surveys of all of the Board's operations. In 1945 Dr. Gill went to South America, where he spent two years studying the needs of various fields and planning with the missionaries for the future. In January, 1946, Dr. Sadler went to Europe, giving special attention to the Balkan States, and to the Near East. In 1947 he spent time in Nigeria, where already Dr. I. N. Patterson, superintendent of the mission, was engaged in a new survey of needs. Dr. Rankin went to Hawaii in April, 1946, to confer with the workers in the new field. In July he went with Dr. Cauthen, the recently appointed secretary for the Orient, to China, where he spent three months. Together they traveled more than eight thousand miles, studying the manifold task of resettling workers, relief, reconstruction, and rehabilitation of schools and churches. He could not get clearance to go to Japan, but Dr. Cauthen was able to go in 1947. With missionary Edwin Dozier he made a careful study of the new situation there, out of which came a call for sixty new missionaries and a half-million dollars for enlargement.

Out of these surveys came facts which served as the basis for an enlarged program in every area and extension to new areas. In Latin America, Guatemala, Honduras, and Venezuela were marked for future missionary appointees, in addition to the seven countries already occupied. In Africa work was extended to the Gold Coast (now Ghana) and Southern Rhodesia. In the Near East work was projected in Transjordan and southern Arabia. By the end of 1947 the work in Japan was reinforced, and the rehabilitation of churches was well under way; and in China all the stations had been reoccupied, except in sections of North China and Manchuria which were held by the Chinese Communists. The 504 missionaries under appointment for nineteen countries had become 623 for twenty-five countries or national areas.

The only serious interruption of the new pace of Southern Baptist missions came in China with the victory of the Communists over the National Chinese government, which was transferred to Formosa (Taiwan) in 1950. Again our missionaries were forced out. But even that calamity was not all tragedy; there were other fields to be occupied. Some of the missionaries went to Japan, by that time wide open for the gospel; some settled in Hong Kong, where work had begun to flourish; some went to Formosa; some to Korea, the Philippines, and Hawaii; and others to fields in Thailand, Malaya, and Indonesia, to establish entirely new work. The spirit of the enterprise was not interrupted. The closing of one road only brought search for another. The sense of mission to a lost world held. And at the end of 1953, the year of Dr. Rankin's death, the number of missionaries had grown to 908 and the number of national areas of the enterprise to thirty-four.

It would be impossible to measure the fruits of the enterprise from year to year. It would require the record of the work of every missionary and of every person won to Christ, of every church as it reached out into each community with its witness and ministry. It would include the transformation brought in family and social life. It would have to follow the Bibles and other Christian literature into thousands of hearts and homes. It would tell the story of compassion and healing in Christian hospitals. Statistics recorded in the annual of the Southern Baptist Convention are eloquent of faithful and growing enterprise.

Every year thousands of new converts were received into the churches by baptism, more than 120,000 between 1946 and 1953. More than five hundred new churches were organized, and the programs of the churches in evangelism,

Bible teaching, and Christian training were expanded. In 1953 there were 697 young men studying for the ministry in nineteen seminaries; and in 580 other schools, from kindergarten to college, were more than sixty thousand students. Nine publishing houses in as many different countries distributed 51,000 Bibles, more than a half-million books, 1,300,000 magazines, and 6,000,000 pamphlets. And in eight hospitals more than 187,000 persons were treated.

Dr. Rankin was more than an administrative leader. He was conscious from the first that the growth of the enterprise abroad depended upon the spirit and purpose of the denomination at home, which in turn depended upon their understanding of the spirit and purpose of the Board and the missionaries in the world venture. His concern, therefore, was to interpret to the denomination the objectives, policies, and operations of the Board.

Vast numbers of Southern Baptists still pictured the missionaries in a pioneer frame, engaging in a small and simple enterprise of witnessing personally to the lost, distributing tracts and Bibles, and preaching to simple and ignorant people. In some pioneer fields missionaries did encounter such situations and tasks. But in Latin America, Africa, China, Japan, and other lands the reality embraced much more. And Dr. Rankin was always trying to paint the missionary picture in a larger frame and on a different background. The darker colors of spiritual darkness, of paganism and perdition are still predominant in the background. The faces of millions and millions of bewildered and despairing lost men are there. The missionary is more conscious of that than of anything else in his environment, and his primary objective is the winning of these millions to Christ for their redemption. If there were not this darkness, he would not be there; and as long as it is there he must be there with the light of the gospel.

But there are other features in bright colors. There are the increasing numbers of the saved. And what are they doing? Dr. Rankin summarizes the picture: "These people who have been saved organize themselves into churches; the churches organize themselves into Baptist associations and conventions. Through their associations and conventions they project programs of Christian missions and evangelism, education, medical work, publication and other forms of Christian service (just as we are doing here in the South)." They are building a Baptist denominational life.

And what is the missionary's relation to them? What is the objective of the Foreign Mission Board among them? The answer is that the Foreign Mission Board is *assisting* these Baptist churches in conducting all the types of activities promoted by the Southern Baptist Convention here at home —churches, mission boards, schools, publication houses, hospitals, women's work, and so forth; and the missionaries are a part in the development of these programs. The objective is to help them until they can do it without us and win their lands to Christ. The picture is that of an entire denominational undertaking in each of more than a score of countries! Is this a small and simple task, calling for only a marginal concern and the "leftovers" from our opulent table?

This picture of a ministry to the Baptists of other lands— to be compared with United States aid to other countries today—was drawn in tones of complete unselfishness and in the bold strokes of our Baptist faith in individual responsibility, local church autonomy, and Christian brotherhood. It represents Baptist faith at its best, promoting the growth of other Baptist churches as we promote our own.

Dr. Rankin welcomed the many questions that came to his office about the affairs of the Board. He felt that good public relations required that they be answered candidly and constructively. They concerned such things as the appointment of missionaries and the kind of persons that should be appointed, the salaries of missionaries and secretaries, endowments, the size of the reserve fund and why it was not spent to meet the pressing needs, the percentage of the missionary dollar that finally reached the field, policies of the Board in respect to co-operation and the ecumenical movement, the secretary's personal views on many things. Sometimes the inquiries were from friends who wanted to be helpful—editors or pastors who wanted to clear up misunderstandings. Sometimes they were frankly critical and sometimes simply curious. In every instance Dr. Rankin's reply was appreciative and frank. If he received the impression that the questions were widely entertained, he was careful to clear them up in the articles he was constantly writing for the *Commission,* Baptist papers, Sunday school literature, the layman's magazine, or in special pamphlets. If the question was not general, he let a personal letter suffice.

In every instance of controversy within the Convention many wanted to know the position of the denominational secretaries and the boards. For example, Dr. Rankin received at one point a number of inquiries about his position on "close communion" and "alien immersion." His reply to one of these questions is sufficient to indicate his wisdom and his deep concern for our basic Baptist principles:

Unfortunately, those of us who serve as secretaries of the agencies of the Southern Baptist Convention, cannot speak on matters that are controversial without involving the agencies with which we serve. As you have indicated in your letter, churches in the Southern Baptist Convention hold varying positions concerning the ordinances of baptism and the Lord's Supper, particularly with reference to practices which are ordinarily indicated by the terms "close communion" and "alien immersion." So far as I know, the Southern Baptist Convention as such has never attempted to define the positions which churches should take in these matters. Since the Foreign Mission Board represents all of the churches of the Southern Baptist Convention, I question whether a secretary of the Foreign Mission Board has the authority to inject an agency of the Convention into a discussion of questions concerning which the Convention itself has not taken specific position.

For the above reason, I do not think it would be for the best interest of the Foreign Mission Board or of our relationship to the churches of the Southern Baptist Convention for me to be quoted in a statement concerning these questions. I fully appreciate, however, your desire and motive in seeking to secure as much information along these lines as you can.

The most pronounced belief and practice among Baptists as I have known them in the South is the sovereignty of each local church and the conviction that no convention has Biblical authority to determine the practices of individual churches. It is on this point that I have become distinctly concerned about developing trends among Southern Baptists. I am particularly concerned about whether or not the Southern Baptist Convention is to be changed from a convention of churches into an ecclesiastical body which legislates for churches. As someone has recently said, the Convention cannot be an organization or agency to tell churches what they can or cannot do. The churches tell the Convention what it can do. We have among us those who speak of actions taken by the Convention as "solemn enactments."

If our state conventions and the Southern Baptist Convention are to remain as agencies in and through which local churches cooperate in undertakings which the churches cannot carry out individually, allowances must be made in such cooperation for individual differences. I believe we can bring disaster to ourselves as Baptists by taking either one of two extreme positions. On the one hand, we can go to such an extreme in accepting any and all kinds of individual differences in faith and practice that we shall have little in common in our faith. Such a course would eventually destroy the very faith which we profess to believe. On the other hand, we can go so far in seeking through our conventions to regulate and legislate every detail of faith and practice of individual churches that these churches can no longer be independent but become the property, spiritually and intellectually, of an ecclesiastical body. Such a course would completely destroy the faith we call Baptist. We must find our way between these extremes. In dealing with the most perfect of any of us, the good Lord still has to make great allowances for much that is wrong in all of us. He manages to do this without ever compromising His own truth and divine word. Somehow, we must learn to maintain the integrity of our faith in God's Word and, at the same time, make the kind of allowances for the errors and shortcomings of each other that God has to make in dealing with us.

As both you and I have indicated, all through the years churches in the Southern Baptist Convention have differed with reference to both the Lord's Supper and baptism. I do not know of a single church in the Southern Baptist Convention that will accept a member without immersion but we do know of a good many churches that will accept immersed members from other denominations provided these members were immersed as an expression of their spiritual death and resurrection through personal faith in the Lord Jesus Christ as Savior. I believe these differences are among those things which we shall have to leave to individual churches to be worked out in terms of the convictions and beliefs of the local members.

To another letter, about the missionary's personal habits, he responded as follows:

In reference to your letter of July 19, I am glad to say that the Foreign Mission Board has never felt it necessary to adopt any regulations concerning the use of tobacco. We try to appoint missionaries who are capable spiritually and otherwise of making their own decisions concerning such matters as this one. Through the years we have never had any serious difficulty in depending upon them in this way. We have found them far more capable from every standpoint in making such decisions for themselves than other people would be in trying to determine what they can do and what they cannot do in reference to a matter like this.

I do not use tobacco myself. I have done so in the past but made my own personal decision, without any kind of pressure from anybody else, for my own personal reasons. I think decidedly that we should grant this same privilege to all other ministers. We have outstandingly able and spiritually powerful men in our Convention who use tobacco. I am sure those men are just as capable of knowing God's will for their lives as I am. I have confidence in them and I am perfectly prepared to let them determine their own response to God in this matter without my attempting to tell them what they should or should not do.

I think we run into serious danger of violating scriptural teachings when we attempt to set up regulations over our fellow Christians. If we start a process of trying to regulate whether or not a man can use tobacco, we might well go ahead and try to determine how many cups of coffee he can drink a day and produce rules that will regulate the minute actions of other people according to the particular ideas that a few individuals have as to what other people should do.

You have asked me for an opinion and I give it to you honestly and sincerely. I am confident that you will not agree with the opinions I have given. I respect you entirely in the honesty and sincerity of your opinion. I can only ask for that same respect for my opinion.

In a large correspondence on various matters, his one purpose was to serve the unity of the denomination for its world task by frankly stating in every case the policy or position of the Board, together with the facts and principles on which it rested. He was confident that clear understanding of the bases of the Board's procedures would elicit from

Southern Baptists the widest confidence and support. He believed that to voice as often as possible such generally held Baptist principles as those cited in the two letters mentioned would do more to achieve true unity and a spirit of brotherhood in the denomination as a whole than any effort at evasion of interpretative differences or at pleasing a particular segment of opinion, whether large or small.

He was as adamant as any in his loyalty to those principles that make us Baptists; he was more tolerant than many of variations in the form and practice which have always been among us. To attempt to subject individuals to an accredited code of conduct, or churches to an authoritarian manual of practice (i.e., to establish a Baptist Church over the churches), is to divide and to cripple the freedom necessary to true spiritual unity. On the other hand, to magnify the underlying principles that make us Baptists and to grant to one another the right of opinion that we claim for ourselves is to create a unity that will free and inspire the denomination to carry its message of faith to the world. This he strongly believed.

In the same spirit Dr. Rankin was concerned that the policies of the Board should be true and wise expressions of our Baptist faith and purpose. A case in point was the method of the Board's educational policy in the British colony of Nigeria. Instead of providing a system of public education, it was the policy of the British Government to collect taxes from the people and provide grants-in-aid for education to voluntary agencies, including religious groups. The only conditions were that the schools should meet required educational standards and be open without discrimination to those who passed competitive entrance examinations. In every other respect the schools were free. The government depended wholly upon them for the education of Nigerian children. Unable to provide for the full support of public schools in the communities of the Baptist churches, and unwilling to leave education wholly in the hands of Mohammedan, Roman Catholic, and other agencies, the Foreign Mission Board in 1926, in the administration of Dr. J. F. Love, agreed that Baptist schools should accept such grants-in-aid "with the understanding that vigilance will be exercised in guarding the principles which Southern Baptists hold dear, and that if at any time there should be an impingement on these, the necessary steps should be taken at once and full information be furnished this Board."

For several years no serious question was raised, since Baptist schools operated with full freedom and without any feeling of conflict with the principle of separation of church and state. It seemed to be simply practical co-operation without compromise of principle. However, in the rapid changes going on in the world the relation of church and state became an acute issue requiring serious reconsideration. In the United States the principle of separation was being endangered seriously in the very field of education. Nigeria was moving toward freedom from English control in its internal affairs, and Baptist leaders saw the possibility of a pagan or Mohammedan rule that probably would not pursue the "hands off" policy of England. The Baptist course had to be re-examined. The Foreign Mission Board was at one with the denomination in that conviction, and in 1950 Dr. Rankin and a commission from the Board went to Nigeria to study the situation and find a solution about which there could be no question of the principle at issue and at the same time find a way for the Board to continue its own program of Christian education.

121

Some Southern Baptists had an easy answer: simply pass a resolution in Richmond abandoning the policy and withdrawing all financial and missionary co-operation with Nigerian Baptists if they were unwilling to follow our lead. But the problem was not so simple as that. That would be to demand immediate and complete severance of Baptists from their schools, in which there were thirty thousand students, without consulting with them. The Nigerian Baptist Convention was an autonomous body of 350 churches and twenty-five thousand members, and the Board felt that in any revision of policy their counsel and willing concurrence should be sought. To ignore their freedom and their judgment, to treat them as a colony of the Southern Baptist Convention, would be to shut the door against future opportunity.

The commission went, therefore, and sat down with Nigerian Baptist leaders to face together the whole situation; and they were able to reach agreements that affirmed the Board's adherence to the separation of church and state and the principle of Baptist freedom and co-operation. They agreed that the Southern Baptist mission and the Nigerian Baptist Convention should "set up a limited system of schools, to be supported, controlled, and operated entirely by Baptists, primarily for the purpose of training Nigerian Baptist workers"; and that these schools should not receive grants-in-aid from the government but would depend for support upon the Nigerian churches and the Foreign Mission Board, which would give them priority in the use of its resources and personnel.

They also recognized "the responsibility of the Nigerian Baptist Convention to make their own decisions with reference to schools that receive grants-in-aid from the government"; that is, our co-operation in the churches and church-supported schools and the Convention would not be conditioned upon their agreement with us in our interpretation of the separation of church and state. This is essentially the same assurance of brotherly co-operation which Dr. Rankin had helped to formulate in China and Japan as responsibility shifted from the Board to the national conventions. The result in Africa has been an increase in Baptist-supported schools, a closer brotherhood, and a great advance in the whole Baptist mission program; at home the feeling was that the solution was a true representation of Baptist principles and a worthy expression of brotherhood among Baptists.

A second case in point was a by-product of the ecumenical movement and the action of the Southern Baptist Convention in refusing to join the Federal Council of Churches (later the National Council). The denomination was solidly against church union. Some, however, wanted to expand the Convention's action into a policy of complete severance from all interdenominational relations. This involved the participation of the Foreign Mission Board in the Foreign Missions Conference of North America. The radical demand for isolation paid no regard to the history, purpose, and value of the conference or to the nature of the co-operation. It was simply a negation of all co-operation with other Christian bodies. The Board and Dr. Rankin stoutly resisted this demand.

A few openly accused Dr. Rankin and others of trying to lead the denomination into the Church Union Movement, utterly disregarding Dr. Rankin's known position on that subject and his record as a Baptist in interdenominational associations. He was not an isolationist, but he was always a Baptist. In his early missionary experiences and studies he had come to see the mutual benefit that Christians of various affiliations could be to one another by counseling together about their common task of winning the world to Christ. As a young missionary he had represented the Leung Kwang Baptist Association more than once in the National Christian Council of China. He had attended the World Mission Conference at Madras (1939) as a delegate of Chinese Christians. After becoming executive secretary, he actively participated in the meetings of the Foreign Missions Conference and served on important committees. He saw many values in these associations.

He also became conscious of the limitations of co-operation and the necessity of freedom for every denomination in making its own program and voicing its own message. He resisted any action that demanded the abandonment of these freedoms. No man believed more deeply in our Baptist doctrines and principles than he; no man was bolder in expressing them and defending them whenever they were challenged. He believed in their truth and that the world had need of them—the Christian world and the pagan world alike. He was, therefore, unafraid and willing for Baptists to co-operate with other denominations in matters of common concern, so long as the autonomy and freedom of each to make its own program and proclaim its own message were respected. His description of a Christian as an individual in community applied also to a denomination—it exists in community.

He sought, therefore, a positive rather than a negative approach to the problem of Baptist relations to other Christian bodies. In 1949 he stated his position to the Southern Baptist Convention as follows:

I should like to see a relationship between Southern Baptists and other Christian bodies which will give to those groups the same measure of respect and appreciation that we would like them to give to us. In all such relations we must maintain our full liberty and responsibility to be loyal to our own convictions concerning God's direct approach to the individual through Jesus Christ. In my opinion, we should not hold any relationships that will make us a part of organic ecclesiastical church councils such as the Federal Council or the World Council of Churches.

In holding convictions which make us unwilling to have part in plans and organizations which are seeking to achieve organic church union, we crave the respect and appreciation of those who hold differing convictions. As these other groups seek to be loyal to their beliefs concerning God's leadership in their lives, I should like to see all Southern Baptists give to them the respect, appreciation and Christian goodwill that we desire for ourselves.

I believe that it is possible for us to maintain relationships with other Christian bodies which will manifest this spirit of appreciation and Christian goodwill without involving us in movements for church union. The essence of Christian cooperation is a Christ-like attitude to all of God's children wherever they are to be found. Our inability to have part in cooperative projects which have church union as their objective, should not prevent our earnestly seeking to maintain every relationship that we can use to manifest a Christ-like attitude to other Christian bodies.

The spirit and meaning of this statement appeared in the relation of the Foreign Mission Board to the Foreign Missions Conference of North America, in which Southern Baptists had played an important part for many years. Dr. R. J. Willingham twice served as its chairman. There were no serious problems of co-operation as long as it was simply a conference of free groups; all were conscious of its benefits. The time came, however, when its work took on increasing tendency to follow the line of the organized ecumenical movement to merge all interdenominational movements into one body. Dr. Rankin more than once registered protests, as his correspondence shows, and expressed in the conference his strong dissent from the idea of its becoming any other than a conference. When it became evident early in 1950 that it was to become a part of the National Council of Churches, he did not hesitate to recommend the withdrawal of the Board from membership, nor did the Board hesitate to withdraw. He believed in free co-operation among Christians and that to replace spiritual unity through free association with the demands of corporative unity was to follow a road that would "make divisions among Christians sharper and deeper." The freedom and spiritual unity that Baptists sought among themselves they could not forsake in their relation with others.

From the beginning of his secretaryship Dr. Rankin had one central purpose. Everything else—his administrative ideals for the Board and its missions, his care to keep the denomination informed concerning the policies and missionary activities in the various fields, his effort to interpret the basic faith and principles of Baptists in relation to their mission—was integral to the purpose. He dramatized it in the word "advance." In his meaning it was, first, a summons to expansion and enlargement, having the military ring of "Forward march" and the evangelical challenge of "Onward, Christian soldiers." One of the heaviest burdens of his heart was that Southern Baptists were doing so little for a perishing world, with so much wealth in men and money and so great a gospel to share.

Advance meant also a challenge to new dimensions of depth in understanding, conviction, and dedication to our world task that would make it the central purpose of our existence as a denomination. He began to use the word while he was secretary for the Orient, possibly after having read Dr. Latourette's *Advance Through Storm*. When he became executive secretary, he made it his watchword. It was the one thought he wanted to plant in the minds of Baptists as the command of Christ and the plea of mankind. And, by the grace of God, he was privileged to see the forward movement which already had begun swell into an unprecedented tide of Baptist advance which continues still to grow in spirit and power. He will be remembered among us as the "apostle of advance."

The occasion of the first public expression of his challenge was a centennial address early in 1945. Citing a statement of the Southern Baptist Convention in 1866, when the South lay prostrate after the Civil War, he called upon Southern Baptists to match in their day the faith of their fathers. The fathers had said, "We can discern but one command; we realize but one trust; we are burdened with but one duty; we feel but one desire in this work: Go forward! Through God we will obey." Dr. Rankin's challenge was in that context:

We enter the new century of missionary service in the midst of a war which has brought unparalleled suffering and destruction to the entire world. . . . In all their history Southern Baptists never possessed greater resources than they have now for rendering a world-wide missionary service. . . . At present *five and a half million* Southern Baptists are furnishing only 542 active foreign missionaries (*five and a half hundred*) , and are giving less than three million dollars a year through foreign missions to help meet the needs of a suffering and destitute world. . . . With our resources how many missionaries should we have? How much money should we give? To win the war we have not counted the cost. We give as many men and as much money as are needed. . . . The Foreign Mission Board does not dare to make its plans for the new century with only 542 missionaries. If we do we shall be unworthy of our heritage and we shall fail in the task before us. . . . The time has come for Southern Baptists to stop thinking in terms of small things. We are great in numbers and resources. God is calling us to be great in his service. We must frankly expect great things of ourselves.

The "great things" he proposed as immediate necessities for a worthy program was the addition of two hundred more missionaries, two million dollars for enlargement, two million for rehabilitation, and two million for a protective reserve fund, making 750 missionaries and eight and a half million dollars!

When he dared that early to propose all of this as an immediate goal of advance, some applauded it as an excusable dream of a new and enthusiastic secretary or as Chinese bargaining that would settle for something less. The fact that he proposed no schedule or special campaign eased the shock of the summons. But those who took him lightly did not know the depth of his passion or the strength of his determination.

Although there was substantial increase in personnel and contributions in 1945 ("more than ever before in our history"), he came back, nevertheless, in 1946 to say, "In the light of the world's urgent need, the Foreign Mission Board's present program can be seen in its *tragic smallness*. . . . In view of such a need it is *unthinkable* that we shall continue to send only 550 missionaries to tell the world about Christ; it is unthinkable that we shall continue to give only an average of seventy cents per person per year to help all the world outside our territory." He began to make fresh comparisons between our plenty and the world's poverty, our expenditures at home and our contributions to foreign missions, our crowded pulpits and the thin line of missionaries abroad.

In 1946 sixty-two new missionaries were appointed. In a special offering in July through September the churches gave nearly four million dollars for relief and rehabilitation in the Orient and Europe. The Lottie Moon Offering reached a new high mark with $1,200,000. There were increases also in receipts from the Cooperative Program, and designated gifts amounted to approximately a half-million dollars. The hearts of Southern Baptists were responding to the world's needs, and missions was finding a new level.

A timid soul would have been willing to adjust to the rate of advance that seemed to have set in, but Dr. Rankin was of a different mind. What had been done in 1946 he saw as but an earnest of what the denomination would do if the Foreign Mission Board would set the goal. In April, 1947, he said in his report to the Board:

> The time has come for us to challenge Southern Baptists with the outline of a program of missions commensurate with the faith that six million Baptists profess and the potential resources we possess. Such a program, even in minimum outline, will be so vastly larger than anything we have ever seriously contemplated that it will be startling. Even so, the time has come for us to hold up that kind of program before our people.

In the Board there was little difficulty in agreeing in principle, and the secretary was given encouragement to pursue the idea and work out a concrete expression of the challenge.

For the rest of that year much time was given by Dr. Rankin and the other secretaries and staff members to gathering data from the fields and the home situation. Already careful surveys had been made or were in progress. Dr. Gill had spent two years studying the Latin American situation; Dr. Sadler had spent much time in Africa, Europe, and the

Near East; and Dr. Cauthen had led in a similar survey of the needs and opportunities in postwar China and Japan. On January 1, 1948, Dr. Rankin and the other secretaries of the Board went to a quiet place outside of Richmond, where they could work without interruption, and spent three days in formulating a plan of advance. Armed with world maps, mission reports, surveys, outlines of suggestions, and in a spirit of prayer, they worked out a plan which they felt would set forward our missionary enterprise in a worthy manner.

In April it was presented to the Board as a program for adoption, calling for continuous advance. It was not to be a special campaign for one or two years or for men and money in a particular period of time. It proposed to reach the goal of 1750 missionaries and ten million dollars a year by a steady and determined march; this was to be achieved as soon as resources could be found. The figures were not chosen arbitrarily but upon the basis of Southern Baptist resources and an estimate of the needs for missionaries in the various fields. They were accompanied by detailed outlines of how and where the increase could be used effectively. It was a proposal to get away from a hand-to-mouth, year-by-year program and to set every year's work in the context of a definite and challenging goal.

The Advance Program was accepted by the Board, to be presented to the Southern Baptist Convention in May. Before the Convention there were strong reactions, not all favorable, to the Board's announcement of so ambitious a project. Some challenged the authority of the Board to launch such a program without the consent of the Convention. In state and Southwide agencies there was fear that it would wreck the Cooperative Program if it succeeded. Some said it would interfere with the state programs for their institutions; others, that it was reckless, thoughtless of other interests, impossible, a dream, fantastic! Some threatened to have it blocked.

But the men at Richmond had not been "reckless"; they had reckoned with the Baptist faith, with the need of the world, with the resources of Southern Baptists not yet tapped, with the rising compassion and concern manifested in the rising tide of contributions in recent years. It was with an unperturbed spirit that Dr. Rankin presented it to the Convention in May on Foreign Missions Night. Beforehand he had sent a copy of the proposed program with a letter to each member of the Convention's Executive Committee, explaining why the Board thought it necessary and urgent and pointing out that it suggested no temporary or special campaign. It had to be based on long-range plans that would provide permanent support through future years.

He also noted that it was projected with not only foreign missions in mind but the whole denominational program; it would necessitate the strengthening and enlargement of the entire denominational undertaking, beginning with the local churches and extending through state and Southwide agencies. It could not succeed if other agencies were left behind. He also called attention to the fact that the Board was conscious that it could be carried out only if, through the Executive Committee, a place was made for it; and instead of recommending a way of implementation, the Board was depending upon the Executive Committee. There was nothing schismatic about it; it was a leap of faith, open-eyed and full of hope.

After its presentation to the Convention, it was referred to the Executive Committee. In his Convention address Dr.

Rankin expressed a deep appreciation of the difficulties the Committee faced in finding a way of advance and spoke of confidence in their resourcefulness once they were convinced. Objection and fears continued. So did Dr. Rankin's effort to convince Southern Baptists that the advance must be done in loyalty to the world purpose of Christ. Contributions to foreign missions could not be pegged at the present level or rate of increase. There must be some way in the Convention financial plan for the vision and compassion of the people to be expressed without "getting out of line." Someone remarked about him in that period of discussion that "Theron was at his best when he had to be stubborn in a great cause."

The Executive Committee proved its vision and resourcefulness when, at the next meeting of the Convention in 1949, it presented a plan which made it possible for foreign missions to advance as far and as rapidly as the people wanted. It proposed a bracketed budget for 1950 in which four million dollars was allocated for current operating expenses of the several agencies, including 50 per cent for the Foreign Mission Board; two and a half million was designated for capital needs of the agencies; and all above this six and a half million would be given to the Foreign Mission Board. And that pattern has been followed since that time, the Home Mission Board receiving 25 per cent of the third bracket after 1950.

The results have revealed what seemed fantastic and reckless to be the wisdom of faith. The first year (1950) yielded through this excess more than $600,000. At this writing, October, 1957, the Executive Committee office in Nashville has just announced that the first two brackets of the budget—*eleven million dollars*—have been reached and that all receipts from October 9 to December 31 will go to missions;

132

this now is called the Advance section of the budget! Not only the Foreign Board but every agency is reaping the abounding fruits of advance.

The Advance Program was given a place within the Co-operative Program. It could succeed only as the total program succeeded. That is exactly what Dr. Rankin and the Board desired. Two words expressed the secretary's thought —"tension" and "balance." The first had reference to the Board's program. In his first report to the Convention in 1945 he said, "We must keep a healthy tension between the forward-moving program [of the postwar period] and a sound basis of financial support." Advance depends on increased support, and increased support can be obtained only by the pull of an advance program. The other word, "balance," had reference to the relation of the Board's program to the program of the denomination at home. They were integral in the world mission of the denomination and had to seek that balance and proportion that would serve the interests of that one mission. The new budgetary arrangement was itself an advance in unity and a prophecy of progress.

The next three and a half years were spent in an effort to feed the fires of Christian compassion, to lift horizons, and to consolidate the denomination in the purpose of continuous healthy advance. The victory sought was still to be. The achievement of the purpose of Christ in the world was in the far distance. In his last report to the Board in April, 1953, Dr. Rankin threw down what turned out to be his final challenge:

I believe God has brought world Christianity to the door of a new era of advance in the coming of his kingdom among men.

133

Do we dare follow him on through the door? Unless we are able to expand our present boundaries of thinking and action concerning God's kingdom, we had better not dare. The world of men in which God is moving today is expecting and demanding far more than can be produced by the token services which organized Christianity has become accustomed to render in the name of our God, who is giving all of himself in Christ for the world.

These forces of advance have been stirring among Southern Baptists. Already they have carried us farther than many of us dared to hope. But it is becoming evident that we have advanced only to the door, where we are seeing the world in a new way. Plans and achievements which we have thought of as being large now appear to be small. We can no longer think that ten million dollars is a great amount of money. A few years ago we thought of one thousand missionaries as being an almost unattainable goal, but not so today.

The significant thing is that our people in the churches are seeing and thinking these things today. They are saying that we have only begun to advance. They can take us far if we will only go with them. Do we dare? If we don't we had better start trying to turn back these currents of advance coming up from Southern Baptist churches. If we do, we had better start increasing the dimensions of our own thinking here in the Foreign Mission Board. Do we dare keep on growing?

Pointing out the reasonable fear of overextending in a time of easy money and insisting that we guard against it by wise caution and a sufficient reserve, he concluded, "But I have another fear. I am much more afraid of standing at the door of the new day of advance in the coming of God's kingdom and of having God pass me by as he moves on, seeking those who will dare to follow him out into the world of this day. I would not *dare* be left standing there!"

He went to the Convention in May, 1953, with that fear and still some misgivings about the extent and wholeheartedness of the commitment to the world task. But on the way home he said to Mrs. Rankin, "I believe it has caught on. I am satisfied. For the first time I feel that I can lay down my work with complete satisfaction about the Advance Program." Little did he dream that in a few short weeks he would take his leave.

On May 21, preparatory to sailing for South America on May 30, he went to his doctor for a physical examination. His general condition warranted a health certificate, but to be perfectly sure, the doctor wished to examine his blood more thoroughly. The next morning the doctor called, asking Dr. and Mrs. Rankin to come to his office. In reply to Dr. Rankin's direct question, "Is it leukemia?" he answered, "It is. You have a right to know." Less than a half-hour later Dr. Rankin led in the staff prayer meeting in the Board's chapel, giving no hint of what he had just learned. Further examinations in Richmond and Baltimore confirmed the first diagnosis.

Not knowing whether he had weeks or months, he continued his work as long as he had strength. He attended the June Board meeting and, as usual, gave the charge to newly-appointed missionaries. Only on his physician's orders did he drop his plan to go to Ridgecrest, where he had hoped to do some writing. Instead he and the family sought a place for rest near by on the Potomac. On June 20 his condition became worse and they returned to Richmond, where a week later, on June 27, he passed in the early morning.

Those last five weeks were faced with the same calmness, courage, and self-possession with which he had more than once faced adversity and change, except that now there was no fear. Once again he proved the meaning of Paul's statement, "I can do all things in him who strengthens me." Those who visited him near the end saw a man facing death. To one he said, "I shall not be able to write any more articles for the *Commission,* but I want to discuss with you something I have been thinking about so that you can write for me." To another, "I have just been reading Buber's *I and Thou* and am thrilled by it." To another who spoke of the many who were praying for him, he expressed his gratitude and added, "It is more important that the will of God be done than that their prayers be answered in the way they want them to be." Thus he died, accepting death with less perturbation than he had experienced when he was asked to leave the Orient for service in the homeland.

After a funeral service in the First Baptist Church of Richmond, in which prayer was offered by his predecessor, Dr. C. E. Maddry, and brief tributes given by his pastor, Dr. Theodore Adams, and by his close friend, Dr. J. B. Weatherspoon, his body was laid to rest beneath the trees of beautiful Hollywood Cemetery in the afternoon of June 29, 1953. In millions of hearts around the world there was weeping and rejoicing that day—weeping over the loss of a proven friend and a great missionary leader who had poured out his life in love for Christ and the world, and rejoicing in the fruits of his work and in the grace of God who had given him to serve in our day and teach us more of the meaning of following Christ. In the weeks that followed, Mrs. Rankin and their daughters received letters from all parts of the world, from Christians of many races and creeds, from simple folk and famous men, all speaking of the same grief and the same gratitude.

So well-known and well-beloved a man needs no other monument than the life he lived, no other praise than the work he accomplished, no other portraiture than the character and spirit and purpose that showed in all his ministry. He had one ambition and that not for himself, and he pursued it with all his heart: it was to serve Christ in his world purpose. It was for that that he committed himself so wholeheartedly to every stage and assignment of his long career. As a teacher he gave himself to learn truth, men and the time in which they lived, and the relevance of truth to life. As an administrator he was committed to the best practices of good business enterprise. As an interpreter of missions and the faith of Baptists he laid a firm grasp on our fundamental doctrines and principles, and it made him a trustworthy leader among us and a trustworthy spokesman for us. He had a respect for persons that made him tolerant of others in their differences and a loyalty to truth that made him adamant in his basic convictions. As an apostle of advance he was intrepid in his challenge and was able to awaken our denomination to its resources and to the centrality of its missionary calling. As a leader in missionary thought and strategy he was recognized as a statesman of the highest order. All of this he was because, like Paul, he was a slave of Jesus Christ, wanting nothing but to be like him and to do his will. Having known Theron Rankin as a person and followed him as a servant of Christ, one dares to say that he had the right and the faith to say again with Paul, "I have fought a good fight, I have finished my course, I have kept the faith: henceforth there is laid up for me a crown of righteousness, which the Lord, the righteous judge, shall give me at that day: and not to me only, but unto all them also that love his appearing."